Westminster Tales

WESTMINSTER TALES

The Twenty-first-century Crisis in British
Political Journalism

Steven Barnett and Ivor Gaber

CONTINUUM
London and New York

Continuum
The Tower Building, 11 York Road, London SE1 7NX
370 Lexington Avenue, New York, NY 10017

First published 2001

British Library Cataloguing-in-Publication Data
A catalogue record for this book is available from the British Library.

ISBN 0-8264-5021-0 (hardback)
      0-8264-5020-2 (paperback)

Library of Congress Cataloging-in-Publication Data
Barnett, Steven, 1946–
   Westminster tales : the twenty-first-century crisis in political journalism
/Steven Barnett and Ivor Gaber.
      p. cm.
   Includes bibliographical references and index.
   ISBN 0-8264-5021-0 — ISBN 0-8264-5020-2 (pbk).
   1. Press and politics—Great Britain. 2. Journalism—Political
aspects—Great Britain. I. Gaber, Ivor. II. Title.
   PN5124.P6 B38 2001
   070.4'49324'0941—dc21

                                                                    00-064519

Typeset by YHT Ltd, London
Printed and bound in Great Britain by Biddles Ltd, Guildford and King's Lynn

Contents

For Zoë
(aged 6 and conceived about the same time as this book)

For Jane
for her constant support

Introduction and acknowledgements

Any book about the media at the beginning of the twenty-first century faces an intractable problem: within months of publication – and in some cases even before it appears – important facts or evidence will be rendered meaningless by the relentless march of, to adapt Harold Macmillan's phrase, 'events'. Such events may involve a new generation of communications technology, another media conglomerate emerging from some corporate merger or takeover, a new piece of communications legislation, or the result of a Law Lords or Brussels ruling.

Even as this book was about to be dispatched to the publishers, the Trade and Industry secretary Stephen Byers gave the green light for a merger of two of Britain's biggest media companies, Carlton Communications and United News and Media. This announcement fuelled speculation about how long it would be before ITV, Britain's first and most popular commercial television network which had originally been a federation of fifteen different companies, was owned and run by a single corporation. Those fifteen companies had gradually merged until there were only three owners: Carlton, United and Granada. Byers' announcement set the stage for prolonged negotiations and possibly a bloody takeover battle, with highly uncertain outcomes.

At the same time, the government was in the middle of a root-and-branch review of the regulatory framework for communications. Under discussion were such fundamental issues as whether the BBC should continue to have its own regulatory structure independent of the commercial sector. The dominant view was that a new 'super-regulator' should encompass all aspects of the broadcasting industry, including content, distribution and competition issues and that this umbrella organization should embrace the BBC. Although the BBC charter lasts until 2005, the whole purpose of public service broadcasting, the funding of the BBC, and whether it could still justify its place in a 'multi-channel society', was yet again a major source of political (and academic) inquiry. A new communications act which will address all these issues is likely to be on the statute books by 2002. In the event, when the White Paper was published in December 2000, the BBC was spared – at least for the moment.

Meanwhile, new technologies were continuing to provoke discussion about 'convergence' (a much-used though ill-defined term) and whether, in the light of ever more inventive methods of electronic data transmission, it was even realistic to talk in terms of 'television' or 'newspapers'. Mobile telephone operators bid in excess of £20 billion for the privilege of owning frequencies on which they hope over the next few years to run lucrative information and entertainment services, while WAP (Wireless Application Protocol) mobile phones are already capable of sending and receiving e-mails and connection to the Internet and a new generation of even more powerful (3G) mobile phones is soon to be launched. The Internet itself is continuing to make inroads into people's homes, offering another source of real-time information, while telephone and cable companies are vying with each other to offer on-demand services via powerful broadband distribution networks. While innovations such as newspapers available on computer and television programmes downloaded onto mobile phones have led to exaggerated claims about media growing into an indeterminate electronic mass, it is undoubtedly true that news consumption patterns are gradually shifting. Newspapers, in particular, are worried about electronic threats to their viability, and every broadsheet has started to develop new electronic versions (which are now being scaled back as the dotcom mania starts to fade).

While new technology changes the landscape of what is available, the law continues to change the parameters of what is permissible – or obligatory. We have yet to see the impact of The Human Rights Act on such issues as privacy: the nature of some of the more intrusive and personal political reporting could be challenged as a result. And we have yet to see whether the Independent Television Commission will continue to insist that ITV maintains a news bulletin at 10 o'clock now that the BBC news has been moved to the same time.

Superimposed on all these uncertainties of the media scene have been throughout 1999 and 2000 a succession of 'breaking stories' about the way politics is mediated. In particular, there have been a rising number of complaints about what Opposition leader William Hague called, in July 2000, 'government by photo-call and government by spin'. The same month saw a television programme devoted to Prime Minister Tony Blair's official spokesman, Alastair Campbell, against whom much of the criticism about a government obsessed by image and presentation has been directed. In the weeks preceding the programme it was announced that Campbell would take more of a backstage 'strategic' role, leaving his less controversial deputy to handle most day-to-day contact with the press. And in the week immediately following the programme, an internal memo written by the Prime Minister himself was leaked which talked about 'a sense that the Government . . . are somehow out of touch with gut British instincts'. Much of the memo talked about 'perception' and the need for a strategic 'message'. Perhaps the most damaging part was on crime, where Blair wrote, 'as ever, we are lacking a tough public message along with the strategy. We should think now of an initiative, e.g. locking up street muggers. Something tough, with immediate bite which sends a message through the system.' This was precisely the kind of gimmicky approach to government policy that critics had been saying was beginning to undermine the Blair government. It was combined with a concerted attack by some political journalists on Campbell's style, with such veterans as the *Telegraph*'s George Jones writing on 5 July 2000:

> In my 26 years as a lobby correspondent . . . I cannot remember a time like this. There is a vacuum at the heart of the Government's public relations machine. The whole argument over spin suddenly seems about to consume its creators, like some deranged Frankenstein's monster.

Six months later, Jones's prediction seemed to come eerily close to reality with the departure from government office for the second time of Peter Mandelson, the man credited with virtually inventing the Labour Party's sophisticated approach to political communication as Director of Communications between 1985 and 1990. He was forced to fall on his sword in January 2001 over a matter that was as much presentation as politics. It concerned the role he had played in the application for a British passport being made by an Indian businessman who was facing charges of corruption back in India. Mandelson, seen by many as the spiritual founder of 'New Labour', had left himself vulnerable to the charge that he had *appeared* to act improperly and was forced to resign from his post of Northern Ireland Secretary.

We are not the first to observe that modern politics is increasingly becoming a self-reflective whirlwind in which media debates about image versus reality are replacing traditional debates about tax cuts or penal policy. On a number of occasions since the election of 1997, Britain has had a government deemed by the media to be 'in trouble' because its streamlined and sophisticated media operation was incapable of controlling the media, which continued to portray it as 'in trouble' because . . . Alice would have found the logic easier to follow in Wonderland. Nevertheless, there is a real sense among some observers that the notion of 'spin' for Blair's Labour government is in danger of becoming a genuinely disabling political issue, much as 'sleaze' became for John Major's Conservative government from 1992 to 1997.

Such controversies about presentation and the role of the 'spin doctor' have become part of a burgeoning publication industry, but form only a part of this book. While both politics and the media are changing rapidly, we believe there are certain arguments about the changing practice of political journalism which are not ephemeral and will not be rendered obsolete by the next big media merger, new technology invention, Law Lords pronouncement, or damaging revelation about the influence of marketing techniques. The professionalization of political party communication strategies, as many others have noted, has been proceeding for some time and is only one of the reasons why we believe that there is a profound problem at the heart of modern political journalism. Although this book is written on the basis of our own and our interviewees' experience of the UK, we believe that its central argument can be generalized to almost any industrialized democratic society with a mixed media system. We also believe that the arguments contained within it will withstand the uncertainties inherent in the media and political world of the next five to ten years. Part of our confidence stems from our own immersion in the worlds which this book reflects, and the fact that the arguments have been sustained over the four years in which the interviews have been done and the book written.

Inevitably, over such a long period of time, there are a number of people to whom we owe a debt of gratitude, and it would be impossible to list them all here. In particular, we would like to thank those political journalists who talked to us, most of whom have now moved from their original jobs (in some cases twice!) since we interviewed them. In no particular order, they were Andrew Grice, John Pienaar, Henry McRory, Trevor Kavanagh, David Wastell, Nicholas Watt, David Hencke, Colin Brown, Kevin Maguire, Anne Perkins, Patrick Wintour, Lucy Ward, Gavin Partington, Chris Wickham, Julian Hall, Andrew Sparrow, Carole Walker, Adam Boulton and Michael Brunson and others who specifically requested anonymity. Thanks are also due to Sam Lay of Goldsmiths College who conducted many of the interviews. We are also grateful to Christine Geraghty, Joy Johnson, Colin Seymour-Ure and Jay Blumler for their comments, ideas and generally stimulating conversations around this area. As usual, we take full responsibility for any errors of fact or interpretation which have escaped through the net. Particular thanks should go to our publishers, who, during the gestation period, also went through a metamorphosis from Cassell to Continuum. They stuck with us when others might have given up, and we are grateful in particular for the support of Caroline Wintersgill in seeing this project through to the end. Finally, thanks should go to our long-suffering families, who will no doubt be as pleased as us that the task is complete.

they have changed, and how they interact to define the nature of political reporting at the beginning of the twenty-first century. Much recent work has concentrated, rightly, on a growing perception that modern political communication is being progressively undermined in a way which could potentially threaten the core values of a democratic society.[5] Various writers have adduced evidence of declining levels of political partipation, knowledge, interest in or commitment to the basic tenets of democracy, as well as the diminishing status of political representatives. Such analyses concentrate as much on the conduct of formal politics, political parties and elected representatives as they do on the practice of journalism, and often attribute the widespread sense of 'crisis' in political communication to political practitioners: the increasingly sophisticated techniques of news management, crisis management, use of political PR and 'spin doctors'.

Our book takes a deliberately one-sided view of the political communication system, concentrating more on the reporting process than on the machinations of governments or parties. By adopting this focus we hope to shift the emphasis of the debate from one about the crisis in political communication to one about a crisis in political journalism. Our thesis is that the interaction of those pressures outlined in general terms by Eldridge is leading inexorably towards a more conformist, less critical reporting environment which is increasingly likely to prove supportive of incumbent governments. This should not be construed either as a massive conspiracy theory – that somehow political reporters are actively colluding with politicians to offer a sanitized, unchallenging view of political reality; or as an indictment of professional competence – that experienced political reporters are no longer capable of doing their job properly. This argument is different from that propounded by some American commentators, for example, that the adversarial and often cynical approach to political coverage by the press threatens to undermine the legitimacy of political institutions – and that 'journalists are the problem here'.[6] We are not arguing for greater cynicism.

Rather, we see the diminution of an informed, coherent and critical approach to reporting politics as the culmination of a number of interacting structural factors over which working journalists have little control. Indeed, it is this increasing loss of independence in pursuit of professional practice that we believe to be the most worrying aspect of contemporary journalism. In the classic sociological dichotomy of 'structure' versus 'agency', we believe that the pendulum has moved (and is still moving) away from the model of journalists as free professional agents towards a model of journalists increasingly beset and hemmed in by an array of different structural demands. Our argument owes more to the tradition of Walter Lippmann in the 1920s and his conviction that the media are 'too frail to carry the whole burden of popular sovereignty'. The press, said Lippman, is 'like the beam of a searchlight that moves restlessly about, bringing one episode and then another out of darkness into vision. Men cannot do the work of the world by this light alone.'[7] To extend this analogy to contemporary media, our argument is that the brightness of the beam is being dimmed and its direction increasingly focused away from the areas that give citizens the kind of informational and critical nourishment they need for a healthy, participative democracy.

Before we introduce the main strands of the argument which form the core of this book, it is important to offer two caveats. First, although our study makes generalizations about not just the present but also the future of political journalism, we must emphasize that the empirical work which underscores it was carried out within a very particular – and highly unusual – political environment in Britain. In the general election of May 1997 the Labour Party achieved a landslide victory which broke several long-standing political records, ended eighteen years of Conservative Party government, and by general consent was a watershed in British politics.

Of the many records broken, the two most pertinent to this book were Labour's overall majority of 179, its largest ever and the largest secured by any party since 1935; and the virtual collapse of Conservative Party support, which at just over 30 per cent of the popular vote was the party's lowest since the Duke of Wellington's defeat just after the Great Reform Act of 1832.[8] In fact, the number of votes actually cast for Labour was half a million *less* than the Conservatives received at the previous election, in which they finished with a slender majority of just 21. It is therefore reasonable to conclude, with Patrick Dunleavy, that there was 'a strong sense in which Labour's apparent strength was just the mirror image of exceptional Conservative weakness'.[9] This electoral context, together with the contrasting popular and parliamentary fortunes of the two major parties, is particularly important when we come to analyse the changing nature of political journalists' relationships with party sources.

The second caveat is that we are cautious about drawing conclusions on the *impact* of this journalistic decline on the body politic or the health of modern democracy. It is clearly not desirable that a significant contributor to the modern public sphere – the mass media – should be increasingly less competent at providing the kind of informative, critical material that citizens require to come to their own judgements about political affairs. There are two reasons why, in itself, this decline need not have catastrophic consequences for modern democracy. First, our argument applies entirely to *mediated* political communication – that is, media output involving material which is uncovered, interpreted, summarized or relayed by third parties (journalists) to their readers, viewers or listeners. It does not address areas of political communication through which citizens have direct access either to relevant information or to their political representatives. As well as covering material routinely available from official sources, this applies increasingly to electronic media forms, which some observers believe might salvage some hope for the future of a healthier political communication system.[10] It also applies to what some American commentators have confusingly called 'new media' (but which in fact are better characterized as new forms of old media): chat shows, phone-ins and interactive programming more generally, which put audiences in direct touch with politicians and which have assumed more significance in recent years.[11]

Second, there is no particular reason for believing that even a mass media system which conforms to the ideal type of public sphere, as envisaged by Habermas and subsequent theorists, would necessarily be exploited or appreciated by citizens who do not immerse themselves willingly in serious and meaningful political discourse. Whatever our aspirations for a universally keen interest and dynamic participation in the process of democracy, the reality is that many – probably most – people are easily bored by politics. This is not a new phenomenon. It was Walter Lippmann, again, who identified back in the 1920s the short attention spans of most people in things political: 'The public will arrive in the middle of the third act and will leave before the last curtain, having stayed just long enough perhaps to decide who is the hero and who the villain of the piece.'[12] While political interest is scarcely likely to be invigorated by a debilitated journalistic culture, the impact of such impoverishment on democracy is perhaps not quite as dramatic as it might have been in a world where, to complete Lippmann's analogy, the public routinely sat through the whole play. On the Enlightenment principle, however, we assume that an independent, critical political journalism is more desirable than a cowed, politically dependent journalism. We have identified four separate but interlocking structural pressures which we think are moving political journalism inexorably from the former state to the latter. Whatever the peculiar political context of the moment, we also believe that these pressures will be unrelieved in the foreseeable future.

The four pressures

The first of these pressures is the changing nature of the relationship between political journalists and formal political sources – in particular, the ways in which greater power is being exercised by government sources to the detriment of other, more informal and less well resourced political sources. As one of our informants told us:

> 'Government spin doctors are very clever. They will work out a strategy for presenting a White Paper and they'll say, "right, we'll give a little bit to the Sundays, another bit to the Mondays and then another bit to the *Today* programme on Wednesday when we launch the White Paper" and there's not much the journalist can do about that, frankly. . . . It's a more sophisticated operation. In some ways we're just seeing a modernization, a more professional approach to it, but I do believe the dangers to democracy are there and the dangers are greater than they were.'[13]

In a sense, this part of our thesis returns us to the 'primary definers' structural position first outlined by Stuart Hall and co-authors over twenty years ago: that certain groups or organizations, through their 'institutional power', are accorded special status and therefore have a strategic advantage in ensuring that their message is prioritized by the media.[14] While Hall *et al.* argued that a number of groups enjoyed the necessary 'accreditation' to exercise influence through the media, we are arguing quite specifically that the centralization and professionalization of formal government and party political information sources now give unprecedented media dominance to the party in power. The same point was powerfully made by Jill Rutter, who shortly after Labour's 1997 election victory was unceremoniously dumped as Chief Information Officer at the Treasury. Commenting on a Cabinet Office report which had examined the workings of the government information machine, Rutter talked of 'the natural advantages of incumbency' in government and expressed some concern that the new government's news operation could become 'a powerful machine to secure the permanent advantages of incumbency'.[15]

We do not believe, therefore, that the dominance being exercised by government is somehow inherent in its power relations with the media; rather, it has been nurtured by understanding and exploiting the way the media work. We therefore agree with Philip Schlesinger that primary definers are not predetermined but learn to be successful 'political entrepreneurs', achieving their aims of media domination through a variety of media-friendly strategies.[16] We seek here to demonstrate the nature of these strategies, how they have become more professional and more widespread and have commanded more resources in recent years, and how such strategies are making it increasingly difficult for even the most experienced political journalists to maintain a critical stance. Although the concept of 'spin doctor' has now become part of the everyday vocabulary of politics, little attempt has been made to unravel the reporting implications of the parties' obsession with 'spinning'.

The second pressure is the impact of media ownership. We are not seeking here to enter the debates about whether the media act, as some have alleged, as a kind of capitalist 'propaganda' conspiracy where media owners are merely ideological agents of ruling elites.[17] Nor are we making judgements about pluralism and whether too many of the most popular and powerful media are concentrated in too few hands, thereby stifling diversity. We are conscious that independent and critical journalism can – in theory – operate even in a privately owned and ideologically committed media corporation, and that '[t]he link between ownership of news organizations and news coverage is not easy to determine'.[18] To sustain the charge that journalists are little more than mouthpieces for their puppet-master owners would require hard empirical evidence which, to our knowledge, has never been adduced in any convincing form. Given the problems with identifying evidence of direct proprietorial control over political reporting, it would be even more problematic to propose a historical shift towards even greater manipulation.

We do, however, believe it is possible to demonstrate two changes in the relationship between ownership and political journalism. First, there is continuing – and possibly increased – willingness of owners to involve themselves in the political process and openly to translate that involvement into interference with journalistic output. The nature of proprietorial interference has certainly changed over the years. In the past, motivation was more explicitly 'political' in the sense of wanting and demanding specific policy outcomes because proprietors deemed them to be 'right': Beaverbrook, for example, wanted free trade for the Empire, Cecil King wanted to get rid of Harold Wilson as Prime Minister. Today's press barons, like Rupert Murdoch and Conrad Black, take a more instrumental view based on their analysis of which party will best serve corporate interests and commercial ambitions. Jeremy Tunstall draws a sharp distinction between the old Press Lord and the new Media Mogul:

> The old style Press Lord (like Northcliffe or Beaverbrook) successfully accumulates newspapers and then less successfully tries to promote specific political policies through newspaper companies. . . . The Media Mogul's driving urge is *acquisition* – to acquire more publications and other media properties and to turn them around from loss into profit. To the mogul it is profits, growth, and financial performance which come first; but political influence is an amusing extra, not least because it may be turned to commercial advantage.[19]

The second change, following directly from this new commercial imperative, is a growing interdependence of media entrepreneurs and political parties for their own respective self-advancements. Senior politicians have become more and more convinced (whether rightly or not) of the power of the media and have therefore sought to create harmonious relationships with a few elite owners. Simultaneously, electronic and market developments in the media have raised important legislative issues (for example, on cross-ownership and pay-TV access) which have made it more imperative for owners seeking government favours to ensure productive relationships with ruling parties. The end result for owners is a political philosophy based more on pragmatism than on ideology. The primary purpose becomes an urgent need not to upset the ruling elite, which in turn is more likely to translate into a 'chilling' effect on what appears in print or on screen. This evolving corporate policy of accommodation rather than disputation applies as much – if not more – to the publicly owned BBC and its relationship with government as to privately owned organizations.

A third pressure on political journalism is the unprecedented growth in media outlets and the impact of this increased competition on political reporting. Journalism has always been a competitive activity, and political journalists in particular have always prided themselves on their ability to break 'exclusive' stories or uncover new angles or perspectives on existing stories. What has changed dramatically during the 1990s is the sheer volume of programmes, column inches and channels available for political news or comment. In broadcasting, in addition to the continuing bulletins on terrestrial channels, there are further bulletins on the fifth free-to-air channel, an expansion of Sunday political programmes, a fifth BBC radio station dedicated to news and sport, and three UK-based satellite channels devoted entirely to news: Sky News, BBC News 24 and ITN News. In print, one estimate puts the increase in newspaper pagination since 1984 at well over 50 per cent on average, and in some cases double.[20] In addition, the growth of online news services (of which the spectacular success of the BBC version is just one manifestation) has added to the news glut.

Such a burgeoning of media output has three effects. First, the volume of material which journalists themselves must now follow and digest to 'keep up' with the news is time-consuming. Combined with the increasing number of outlets many journalists are expected themselves to service – whether it be updated editions of newspapers or the ever-expanding number of news bulletins – there is much less time for the kind of painstaking enquiries or rigorous questioning that a critical approach requires. When time-harried journalists are simultaneously being inundated with press releases and phone calls from well-funded political sources, it becomes more difficult to find the ammunition with which to oppose or deflect the government agenda. We consider the impact on political journalism of this outpouring of political interview programmes in more detail in Chapter 6.

The second effect is the intensification of ratings battles, in which audience size (and to a lesser extent composition) can take precedence over news content. Some scholars have argued on the basis of newsroom studies that professional journalists have little conception of their audience, and have identified a 'missing link between the producers and consumers of news'.[21] The intensifying competition in news provision has focused attention on strategies of audience maximization to the point where, if anything, concern for audience gratification is now eclipsing the influence of core professional news values. The growing practice of running surveys and focus groups, then feeding the results back into newsroom practice and the selection of news stories, has led to a consumerization of news content which gives high priority to notions of 'accessibility' and intrinsic viewer interest. This ratings-led, consumer-led approach to news has been blamed for a more trivialized content which concentrates on show business, crime, scandal, royalty and softer 'lifestyle' stories at the expense of foreign news and issues concerning social and economic policy.[22]

This 'tabloidization' thesis of news provision is generally condemned for producing a less informed, less interested citizenry. In fact, for our thesis, it is not necessary to make any value judgements about whether news is being driven by a titillating, trivializing impetus which results in a politically ignorant electorate (a bad thing) or whether it is shedding a professional elitism about news values which historically succeeded only in alienating audiences from politics (a good thing). Either way, the end result of increased competitive pressure is less time and less space for political reporters to mount serious investigations which will allow them to subject political orthodoxies to proper scrutiny.

The third effect is the greater power that such proliferation of outlets puts into the hands of those who control the flow of information. It is now established practice to release relatively complex but important information close to reporters' deadlines. This ensures that journalists are increasingly dependent on sources not just for the information itself but for the inter-pretation – the 'spin'. As we shall see, it also encourages political sources to

impose conditions on which ministers or spokespeople will make appearances or write articles. Refusals to appear simultaneously with a senior
political opponent, demands for the last word, strict agreements on what
may or may not be covered in an interview have all become a recurrent part
of the political reporting scene. It becomes more difficult for broadcasters, in
particular, to reject such demands when they know that competitors will
happily accede to some of or all the imposed conditions.

The fourth trend is the changing nature of the journalism profession: its
hierarchies, training, use of new technology and employment conditions. We
attempt to construct a coherent picture around a number of different structural changes within the media industries that are tending to militate against
a reporting culture which is thoughtful and challenging, and towards one
which is rushed and conformist. Thus, the introduction of new digital
technologies in broadcasting has given rise to a new breed of multi-skilled
journalists who are expected to research, interview and in some cases edit
and transmit with minimal technical assistance and with enough dexterity to
meet the demands of (sometimes) many news outlets. At the same time,
employment patterns in the media industry have shifted, with relatively
secure full-time jobs giving way to much greater use of freelance and contract
reporting. Although they are often dedicated professionals, these journalists
are more susceptible to the demands of their commissioning editors and
therefore have little scope for moving beyond their specific briefs. Meanwhile, the ephemeral and vulnerable nature of freelancing gives more power
to senior editors in dealing with staff journalists who may want to move
beyond a programme or publication's political remit. In this kind of environment, it takes a courageous political reporter to defy his or her boss.[23]

At the same time, training opportunities for political reporters are in
decline, thereby depriving potential recruits (and their future employers) of
the talents and professional advice of seasoned operators in political journalism. While general courses within university departments abound, the
prospects for on-the-job training on local papers and large institutions such
as the BBC are fading. This too has its consequences for emulating role
models in reporting excellence. In the words of Bob Franklin,

> Amid the current welter of newszak it is still possible to identify the work of
> distinguished journalists . . . but the system which nurtured them, honed their skill
> and offered them opportunities for gaining a wide variety of journalistic experi-
> ence is virtually dead.[24]

It is not our purpose to offer a wholly determinist perspective, nor to be
relentlessly negative in our appraisal of modern reporting of politics. There is
still some measure of independent-minded, well-researched and critical
journalism that succeeds in its intention of discovering and disseminating
information to the public which governments find uncomfortable and which
thereby helps to hold those governments to account. There is still a – fairly –
healthy fourth estate. But for the structural reasons outlined in this book, its

health is in decline and we can see no respite. We believe that the crisis in twenty-first-century political journalism has already begun.

Notes

1. Henry Porter (1985) *Lies, Damned Lies and Some Exclusives*, p. 87. London: Coronet.
2. Quoted in Shanto Iyengar and Richard Reeves (eds) (1997) *Do the Media Govern?*, p. ix. London: Sage.
3. F. S. Siebert, T. Peterson and W. Schramm (1956) *Four Theories of the Press.* Chicago: University of Illinois Press.
4. John Eldridge (ed.) (1993) *Getting the Message: News, Truth and Power.* London: Routledge.
5. Bob Franklin (1994) *Packaging Politics.* London: Arnold; Jay G. Blumler and Michael Gurevitch (1995) *The Crisis of Political Communication.* London: Routledge.
6. Thomas E. Paterson (1993) *Out of Order*, p. 16. New York: Alfred E. Knopf.
7. Walter Lippmann (1984) 'Public opinion', in Doris Graber (ed.) *Media Power in Politics.* Washington, DC: CQ Press. Lippmann expressed similar sentiments in his subsequent book, *The Phantom Public.*
8. Anthony King, David Denver, Iain MacLean, Pippa Norris, Philip Norton, David Sanders and Patrick Seyd (1998) *New Labour Triumphs: Britain at the Polls*, pp. 7-8. Chatham, NJ: Chatham House Publishers.
9. Patrick Dunleavy (1997) 'New times in British politics', in Patrick Dunleavy, Andrew Gamble and Ian Holliday (eds) *Developments in British Politics 5.* London: Macmillan.
10. See, for example, Nicholas Negroponte (1995) *Being Digital.* New York: Hodder and Stoughton, and Roza Tsagarousianou, Damian Tambini and Cathy Bryan (eds) (1998) *Cyberdemocracy: Technology, Cities and Civic Networks.* London: Routledge. We are more sceptical about the potential for 'computer-mediated communications', in particular the dangers of unequal access caused by cost barriers (Steven Barnett (1997) 'New media, old problems: new technology and the political process', *European Journal of Communications*, vol. 12, no. 2, pp. 193–218; Peter Golding (1994) 'Telling stories: sociology, journalism and the informed citizen', *European Journal of Communications*, vol. 9, no. 4, pp. 461–84).
11. In the UK these programmes are particularly common during general election campaigns: for example, *The Granada 500* on ITV gives a representative sample of voters the chance to cross-question politicians, and *Election Call* on BBC exposes leading politicians to calls from members of the public every morning of the campaign.
12. Walter Lippmann (1995) 'The phantom public', in Robert Jackall (ed.) *Propaganda*, p. 48. Basingstoke: Macmillan.
13. Interview with Andrew Grice, January 1998.
14. Stuart Hall, Chas Critcher, Tony Jefferson, John Clarke and Brian Roberts (1978) *Policing the Crisis: Mugging, the State and Law and Order.* London: Macmillan.
15. Speech by Jill Rutter to the Social Market Foundation, London, 4 December 1997. She was referring to the 'Report of the Working Group on the Government Information Service' produced by a Cabinet Office team under Robin Mountfield (the 'Mountfield Report') in November 1997.
16. Philip Schlesinger (1990) 'Rethinking the sociology of journalism: source strategies and the limits of media-centrism', in Marjorie Ferguson (ed.) *Public Communication: The New Imperatives*, p. 79. London: Sage.
17. For example, Edward Herman and Noam Chomsky (1988) *Manufacturing Consent.* New York: Pantheon Books.
18. Michael Schudson (1996) 'The sociology of news production revisited', in J. Curran and M. Gurevitch (eds) *Mass Media and Society*, 2nd edition, p. 144. London: Arnold.
19. Jeremy Tunstall (1996) *Newspaper Power*, pp. 80–1. Oxford: Clarendon Press.
20. Bob Franklin (1997) *Newszak and News Media*, p. 90. London: Arnold.
21. Philip Schlesinger (1987) *Putting 'Reality' Together*, p. 133. London: Methuen. Schlesinger quotes an American study by Herbert Gans in 1966 which came to similar conclusions (p. 115).

22. For example, Franklin, *op. cit.* See also Mort Rosenblum (1993), *Who Stole the News?* New York: John Wiley, for a devastating account of approaches to foreign reporting in the big American networks.

23. A rare example of such courage is the ex-*Daily Mirror* political journalist Paul Foot, who ignored his superiors' demands to stop writing negative stories about the Mirror Group. Since his sacking, the only outlet for his special brand of committed, investigative political reporting is the satirical magazine *Private Eye*.

24. Franklin, *op. cit.*, p. 21.

CHAPTER TWO

Public opinion and the impact of political journalism

Does the content of political journalism actually matter? This might seem a strange question to pose in a book dedicated to investigating the current state of political journalism and the pressures that define it, but such a book carries an implicit assumption: that the way politics is reported in the press, on television and on radio has a material effect both on the individuals exposed to it and on society as a whole. Taken at the individual level, there is an assumption that a simple 'effects model' operates which presumes that individuals are influenced by the political reporting they are exposed to. And taken at the broadest societal level, there is an implicit thesis that 'good' political reporting (however defined) must be beneficial for democracy; and that 'bad' political reporting must somehow be damaging.

Such assumptions need to be made explicit and challenged at both levels before we draw conclusions about the importance of political journalism. Otherwise, at its most extreme, it may well be possible to conclude that the nature of political journalism has been corrupted beyond repair, but that it scarcely matters: either because the body politic is so politically sophisticated that it treats political coverage through the mass media as no more than amusing distraction; or because it is so actively immersed in the political environment through other, more direct means that second-hand consumption of the political world has become almost superfluous. In other words, in theory, the state of political reporting could be immaterial to the state of democratic welfare.

At the societal level, continuing the themes outlined in Chapter 1, we can theorize three contributions that 'good' political journalism might make to democracy. The first – and perhaps the most complex as well as the most problematic – is the relaying of opinions 'on the ground' to policy-making elites, governments and elected representatives; acting, in other words, as tribunes of the people who can convey – through the mass communication process – the distilled consensus of the multitude to its representative lawmakers. The second is information provision: it can convey accurate, intelligible and comprehensive knowledge about contemporary political issues to the electorate, allowing citizens to formulate their own informed responses and – if they choose – to participate accordingly. The third is to contribute to the process of opinion formation: to allow citizens a neutral forum in which to share their views and a space in which discussions can be held and a collective view allowed to evolve. In each case we can try to idealize what 'good' political journalism might consist of, and what its impact might be.

The press as tribune of the people

Looking first at the notion of media as tribunes of the people, the ideal-typical role of political journalists is fairly easy to define. They should be able to act as reflectors of the public mood, both relaying to government the people's concerns and using their privileged access to the mass media to trumpet those concerns and campaign on the people's behalf. This is perhaps easier in the less confining environment of newspaper journalism (particularly populist tabloid papers) than in the world of television and radio, where more attention must be paid to neutrality. There is certainly no shortage of examples of newspapers claiming to be the people's champion, acting as the megaphone of popular dissent and calling on governments, political parties, corporations or other bodies which may have provoked the paper's wrath to 'get something done'.

In practice, of course, this raises a number of problems. On what basis do journalists gauge 'the public mood', and why should their assessment of popular opinion be any more accurate or trustworthy than that of elected Members of Parliament – the constitutional rather than self-appointed tribunes of the people? Can journalists be trusted to set aside the agendas of their newspapers or their personal convictions to interpret the popular will? Indeed, the very notion of interpreting public opinion assumes a simplistic homogeneity in the popular will which allows for no plurality of differing opinions, nor for the validity of contrary minority opinions.

These questions conflate theoretical – indeed philosophical – issues and practical ones. Post-Enlightenment philosophers argued that, in the words of Jeremy Bentham, it was 'the tribunal of public opinion' which prevented abuses of power as governments were obliged to open their decision-making processes to some kind of public scrutiny. While the concept of public opinion is vital to Enlightenment thinking, it in turn raises a number of questions about how that opinion comes to be manifested or understood, and how much weight should be attached in a democracy to 'popular' opinion as opposed to 'representative' opinion.

The tension between these two models of democracy has important implications for the role of the media in general and political journalism in particular. It is a debate with long antecedents, although the arguments in favour of privileging a representative elite over a perceived popular majority are now looking dated. The philosophy was best propounded by Edmund Burke in the late eighteenth century when he argued that, once democratically elected, an MP had a duty to look to interests beyond his immediate constituency, and if necessary to vote and take decisions which were unpopular with constituents if they served some higher national or public interest.

A similar line was taken by one of the founding fathers of American democracy, James Madison, who argued that the 'public good' would be best served by listening to the public's representatives rather than the public itself. Neither position was dismissive of the public's right or ability to involve itself in rational debate and come to a reasoned decision, but both recognized a higher right of representatives to legislate differently rather than feel mandated by majority opinion.

From a slightly different perspective, the journalist who first wrote extensively about public opinion, Walter Lippmann, also endorsed the representative model. For him, the problem was the public's unwillingness to engage with important matters of state for any serious length of time, and hence its tendency to jump to early and ill-considered opinions. The notion that 'when public opinion attempts to govern directly it is either a failure or a tyranny' suggests that the public is capable of a dangerous irrationality which could have dangerous consequences for civic health. At its most extreme, as Schumpeter wrote in the shadow of Nazism, it can result in an emotive populism which tramples individual rights and is fundamentally anti-democratic. For all these thinkers and writers, the fact that such rights can be enshrined within a representative system offered vital protection from a potential 'tyranny of the majority'. A good example in modern legislative history of an elected assembly apparently defying the popular will is the running debate in Britain on capital punishment. It is widely accepted (mainly on the basis of opinion polls) that the majority view is firmly in favour of capital punishment for certain categories of murder or terrorist activity. Repeatedly, however, and after long and careful deliberation in Parliament, MPs have voted to reject it.

A considerable boost for the majoritarian or populist model of democracy came with the arrival of opinion polls. Following his successful prediction of the result of the 1936 presidential election, George Gallup outlined his vision for a totally inclusive democracy in which the mass media would be used to disseminate information and debate throughout the electorate: 'The nation is literally in one great room ... the people, having heard the debate on both sides of every issue, can express their will.'[1] Support for this notion of 'direct democracy' – which by implication downgrades the importance of elected assemblies and prioritizes expressions of majority opinion – has been further increased by new electronic forms of communication which, in theory, allow for interactive voting and expressions of majority opinion. At its most idealistic, this model anticipates a democratic utopia in which the participatory and majoritarian culture of the Greek city-state is reinvented for the modern nation-state. A populist electronic democracy would have both deliberative and plebiscitary advantages, allowing everyone the opportunity to take part in informed debate and then cast their educated vote through the Internet. A version of this view was advanced by two of the most influential writers on new technology and politics, writing for the left-leaning think tank Demos, who recognized the potential for diminishing the role of orthodox political parties and the mass media:

The more utopian advocates of a push-button democracy have argued that widespread access to high capacity telecommunications and databases will enable citizens not only to be much better informed but also to participate directly in decisions. Technology would permit the bypassing not only of parties and parliaments but also of the mass press and broadcasting.[2]

More recently, this technology-led nirvana has been embraced by politicians keen to be associated with images of innovation and modernism. In the United States, it was Vice-President Al Gore who announced his own and his government's enthusiasm for the 'global information infrastructure' and the potential benefits of a technology-led information age. In Britain the Labour government elected in 1997 has combined the rhetoric of new technology with its recently discovered dedication to polls and focus groups. Although originally applied mainly to campaign strategies, these have now been extended into the process of policy development and are employed unapologetically by party strategists determined to portray the government as more voter-friendly and prepared to listen to the 'voice of the people' as distilled through the various mechanisms of consumer research. In policy terms there are fears among some party members that ideology has been replaced by pragmatism, but the more enthusiastic proponents of the new politics prefer to characterize it as a shift towards populism. Peter Mandelson, the architect of Labour's campaigning strategies and twice a senior government minister before his second fall from grace in January 2001, was quite explicit in a speech in 1998:

> 'It may be that the era of pure representative democracy is coming slowly to an end. We entered the twentieth century with a society of elites, with a very distinct class structure. In those days it seemed natural to delegate important decisions to members of the land-owning elite, the industrial elite or the educated elite. When Labour emerged as the party that represented the industrial working class, it developed its own elite of trade union bureaucrats, city bosses and socialist intellectuals. But that age has passed away.
>
> 'Today people want to be more involved. Representative government is being complemented by more direct forms of involvement from the Internet to referendums. Tony Blair's government has already held two referendums and three more are at some stage in prospect. Not to mention more citizens' movements, more action from pressure groups. This requires a different style of politics and we are trying to respond to these changes.'[3]

Setting aside the questionable assumptions about whether citizens do indeed want to be more involved in political activity, this was a clear indication from the heart of government that a new kind of 'electronic democracy' was an inevitable consequence of developments in new technology and was to be encouraged. In fact, recent studies of how computer-mediated communications (CMCs) have been operating in practice tend to show very localized uses which serve an information dissemination function rather than a plebiscitary function. A recent series of comparative investigations in Europe and the United States concluded:

It is striking that, although the initial promise of most electronic democracy projects was to develop and implement interactive local democracy which would enable citizens to express their views, opinions and preferences in binding or consultative polls, this promise has not been fulfilled – at least not to the extent initially anticipated by advocates of electronic democracy.[4]

Optimism on this front is therefore premature – and anyway raises some very serious questions about unequal access and the 'democratic deficit' that arises from the hardware and software costs of going online – but adds to the efficacy of majoritarian arguments. In the absence of any real breakthrough in electronic developments, it means that other ways of identifying the *vox populi* have greater purchase: in particular, opinion polls and the press.

There is no question that the status and ubiquity of the opinion poll have risen with astonishing speed since George Gallup first elevated it from something akin to witchcraft. Although there is no direct empirical evidence, the number of opinion polls published in the press, referred to in public documents or in Parliament, and carried out in confidence by political parties, government departments, local authorities and other bodies charged with representing the public good has risen inexorably over the past fifty years. The most tangible evidence is in electoral campaigning: no study of a presidential or general election is complete without a chapter on the pro-fessional 'pollsters' hired by rival campaigns and their impact on campaigning strategies. Some politicians, however, believe that their influ-ence is more pervasive and insidious: that in the everyday governance of a country, they are beginning to replace political judgement and ideological commitment as politicians genuflect obediently to the 'popular will' as it is conveyed through opinion polls. In a speech in 1996 the former deputy leader of the Labour Party, himself now a respected newspaper columnist, called the opinion poll 'a major disincentive to ideological politics'. He went on:

> 'I want neither to prohibit opinion polling nor to in any way limit its use. I merely observe that its existence and increasing sophistication makes politicians believe that they can choose between principle and popularity. Politicians always thought they knew what the people wanted. Now the newspapers tell them with apparent certainty – tougher on crime, no quarter to the welfare scroungers, keep the blacks out. They can even identify the needs and demands of target voters – help with negative equity, tax cuts and action against incompetent teachers, real and imagi-nary. The newspapers, reflecting their readers' views for commercial as well as ideological reasons, reinforce the popular prejudice. There has never been a time in our history when it was more difficult for a politician to say, "I will lead rather than follow."'[5]

The problem, however, is more profound than the issue of abdicating political responsibility identified by Hattersley. His analysis is a critique of the majoritarian principle of government, but implicitly accepts that the sophisticated apparatus of consumer research is perfectly capable of distill-ing the popular will. In fact, the problem of political cowardice is compounded by the incomplete – and in many cases positively distorted –

nature of public opinion which is actually being distilled. This is not because of any malevolent intent nor even technical incompetence by those organizations which tend to undertake sample surveys (quantitative research) or focus groups (qualitative research). Indeed, in terms of the science of sampling and complex statistical analysis, the legacy of George Gallup (with the help of computer technology) is an extremely professional and sophisticated industry dedicated to the measurement of popular opinion. The problem is neither in the number nor nature of the people being asked their opinion, but the necessarily disengaged nature of opinions being sought.

The vexed question of the 'quality' of measured public opinion is something that has troubled scholars for many years, but rarely raises its head beyond academic journals. And yet, given the growing impact of these widely disseminated measurements, it ought to trouble us that a properly constructed poll will always involve members of the electorate with very little interest in or knowledge of the issues being investigated. The methods of polling are populist in the absolutist sense that everyone's opinion is regarded as equally valid, but take no account of the fickle nature of opinion when unprepared respondents are presented with questions about issues to which they have given very little or no consideration. This is not a paternalistic argument – that disengaged individuals have no right to express an opinion – but a methodological one: opinions solicited without any prior warning or discussion of the issues under discussion are highly susceptible to such vagaries as the wording and order of questions being asked. James Fishkin, who pioneered the notion of 'deliberative polling', which attempts to engage representative groups of electors in relevant debate before ascertaining their opinions, has summarized the problem as follows:

> The movement towards more direct democracy ... in fact results in the decision-making power, in the large nation-state, being brought to a people who are *not a public*. The locus of ostensible decision resides in millions of disconnected and inattentive citizens, who may react to vague impressions of headlines or shrinking soundbites but who have no rational motivation to pay attention so as to achieve a collective engagement with public problems.[6]

Fishkin's analysis neatly identifies the character of the problem as disengaged opinion magnified by the influence of the media. In other words, on issues where individuals do not have any strong feelings or have not been sufficiently concerned to inform themselves beyond a cursory glance at a newspaper or distracted glimpse of a news bulletin, opinions will be more than usually swayed by those media. In such cases, opinion polls reflect not so much the collective views of the citizenry as the most vocally expressed editorial views of the moment being relayed back to the pollsters through the fairly simplistic mechanisms of sample surveys. This critique applies less to the more sophisticated and carefully constructed programmes of attitude research which tend to be conducted by government departments or academics, and more to the kinds of snapshot polls which appear whenever a particularly contentious issue is being debated. The problem is exacerbated

further by the fact that those polls are invariably themselves media-
generated – commissioned by the very programme or newspaper that has a
particular angle of point of view which it wishes to illustrate. The combination of inchoate opinion, inexact techniques and editorial agendas, then,
offers the prospect of newspapers, in particular, using 'measured' public
opinion to reinforce their own editorial views as well as their self-proclaimed
role as tribunes of the people. Public opinion is therefore filtered through
newspapers' own campaigning priorities or political affiliations; they refract
rather than reflect public thinking.

An interesting example of how a number of newspapers claimed to be
interpreting public opinion, while in practice seeing a very complex moral
question through their own perspectives, was the issue of whether homosexual politicians should be 'outed' – that is, revealed as being gay without
their permission. The story arose in October 1998 when the cabinet minister
responsible for Wales, Ron Davies, was the alleged victim of a robbery on
Clapham Common in south London. The circumstances of the robbery were
never made clear, but the fact that Davies admitted to meeting and willingly
going off with a stranger in an area renowned for its casual homosexual
encounters – and the fact that he immediately tendered his resignation –
triggered much sensationalist speculation about his personal life. A day later,
the ex-MP and openly gay political columnist Matthew Parris was being
interviewed on the BBC's late-night news programme *Newsnight* about the
issue of homosexuality in politics and mentioned that there were at least two
gay MPs in the cabinet. Pressed further by a surprised Jeremy Paxman, the
interviewer, Parris named the openly gay Culture Minister Chris Smith and
added that the then Trade Secretary Peter Mandelson was 'certainly' gay. An
unusually flustered Paxman muttered, 'I'm not sure where he stands on that'
and moved swiftly on. This unprompted revelation about a cabinet minister,
particularly someone as high-profile as Mandelson, caused something of a stir,
and was reinforced by a rather heavy-handed memo circulated to BBC
journalists two days later. It ran, 'Please will all programmes note that under
no circumstances whatsoever should the allegation about the private life of
Peter Mandelson be repeated or referred to in any broadcast.' Although simply
reinforcing existing BBC guidelines on reporting of MPs' private lives, such a
personalized approach inevitably extended the shelf-life of the 'story'.

Within a week that story had taken a new twist when another cabinet
minister, Nick Brown, 'voluntarily' came out as homosexual. He had in fact
been threatened with exposure by the *News of the World*, and decided to preempt any tabloid revelations by making a public announcement. He was
given the full support of the Prime Minister and the government. In combination with the Ron Davies and Peter Mandelson stories, the whole question of
'gays in the cabinet' became a hot topic.

At this point the *Sun* felt it appropriate to run a front-page editorial on
behalf of 'the public' which clearly threatened a campaign of outing. Head-
lined 'TELL US THE TRUTH TONY', it was given the ominous sub-headline
'Are we being run by a gay Mafia?' and stated unequivocally that 'the public

has a right to know how many homosexuals occupy positions of high power'. Underlining again its position as a mouthpiece for national concern, it continued, 'there are widespread fears that MPs, even ministers, are beholden to others for reasons other than politics'. The *Sun* even provided – apparently with a straight face – a telephone hotline for 'ministers and MPs who are secretly homosexual' and wanted to come out. While offensive to many, this overtly illiberal approach by the *Sun* was consistent with its attitude throughout the 1980s and 1990s, where it would speak unapologetically about 'poofters' and made no pretence about its distaste for homosexuality. In this respect it reflected the views of its editors and proprietor, Rupert Murdoch. More importantly, the paper believed its attitude was firmly rooted in a widespread sense of public disapproval and intolerance, particularly among its core working-class readership.

The following day, the *Guardian* published the results of an opinion poll which it had commissioned, apparently contradicting the *Sun*'s long-standing view of public intolerance and announcing that 'Exclusive poll shows majority not concerned by homosexuality'. In response to the question 'Do you think homosexuality is morally acceptable or not?', 56 per cent of the Guardian's commissioned opinion poll answered 'yes'. When asked, 'Do you think being openly gay is compatible or incompatible with holding a cabinet post?', 52 per cent said it was compatible. The paper concluded unequivocally that 'the days when it was assumed that the British public was overwhelmingly intolerant of homosexuals are over'.

A day later, the *Sun* performed what was widely seen as a spectacular U-turn. First, it issued a 'new policy statement' declaring that the paper was opposed to the outing of gay politicians. Second, it sacked Matthew Parris, who was a regular *Sun* columnist. Its new policy was explicitly laid out in the following day's leader column: 'From now on the *Sun* will not reveal the sexuality of any gays, men or women, unless we believe it can be defended on the grounds of overwhelming public interest.' Taken with the *Guardian*'s opinion poll, this was widely seen as a triumph for a more progressive public mood over a newspaper's historically bigoted and intolerant editorial approach to homosexuality.

In fact, all was not quite how it seemed. As many commentators pointed out in the days following this editorial volte-face, there were other agendas at work, among them the attitude of the owner of the *Sun*, Rupert Murdoch. There was, first, his daughter Elisabeth's well-known closeness to Peter Mandelson. According to a *Guardian* report, she was 'thought to have complained, with other senior News International executives', about the *Sun*'s position. More importantly, it was Mandelson who would be ultimately responsible for sanctioning News International's proposed and controversial takeover of Manchester United football club. As many observers of the Murdoch empire have observed in the past, his newspapers' editorial positions tend to owe less to a consistently applied ideology than to a pragmatic view of what will further his corporate interests. The *Sun*'s political coverage had been notably friendly towards Mandelson over the previous few months, and it would not have been very politic (or character-istic of Murdoch himself) to offend such a key member of the government. So was the *Sun* bowing to a tide of new liberalism which was sweeping away decades of British prejudice against homosexuality? Or were a few senior editorial staff, under proprietorial pressure, taking out a corporate insurance policy? What exactly was the state of public opinion?

According to one report, many *Sun* reporters maintained that their 'mafia' angle was legitimate because there was still widespread disquiet about homosexuality. The *Guardian* quoted one as saying, 'If you go outside the M25 a lot of people have serious concerns about gays.' This may not have been supported by the *Guardian*'s instant poll, but it is supported by more serious and long-term attitudinal research in Britain. According to the 1996 *British Social Attitudes*, the most authoritative and exhaustive survey research programme of attitudes in the UK, 55 per cent of the population believe that sexual relations between two adults of the same sex are 'always wrong'.[7] The discrepancy between this figure and the *Guardian*'s may be explained by differences in question wording in the two surveys – that being gay is acceptable as long as it doesn't involve sex! – but it raises some awkward questions about newspapers' use of opinion polls in trying to interpret 'public opinion'.

Polls can therefore offer an apparently objective snapshot of the popular view and thus provide the media with an apparently scientific platform for acting as a populist mouthpiece. They are, however, vulnerable to a news-paper's own agenda. Whether or not to commission a poll, the subject matter to be covered, the order and wording of questions – all of which can influence outcomes – can generally be controlled by the newspaper (or television company). At the very least, if results do not correspond with the paper or programme's own agenda, publication can be withheld or relegated to the small print of an inside page. In the end, what the British public really *think* about homosexuality at the end of the millennium is probably unfathomable and certainly unquantifiable. What the British newspapers *wrote* about the public's view on homosexuality in the aftermath of government 'outings' had less to do with trying to gauge true public opinion and much more to do with the newspapers themselves – in this case, the ownership of the *Sun* and the liberal agenda of the *Guardian*.

That newspapers (and indeed television programmes) often have their own agendas should not detract from the argument that the media are capable of articulating the *volonté générale*, and that newspaper political reporters in particular see the representational role as a key element of their professional activity. In describing his paper's campaign against Britain's joining the European Monetary System, the *Sun*'s political editor, Trevor Kavanagh, talked about 'representing 10 million readers' and implied that he and his newspaper had some sort of duty to defend their interests, even against the government if necessary.[8] The whole issue of the single currency is a fascinating example of the complex interrelationships between news-paper agendas, public opinion and the intermediary role of a political reporter. It is certainly true that, when asked to participate in a telephone poll to convey whether they are for or against joining the single currency, vast numbers of *Sun* readers are prone to vote against. This comprehensive expression of collective no confidence, however, invariably follows a blistering front-page account of the dire economic consequences that would follow Britain's entry, and a warning of the European federalism and loss of political sovereignty such a move would entail. The *Sun*'s analysis may or may not be true, but it is difficult to represent the results of these telephone polls as the considered view of its readers when they have been subjected to such one-sided propaganda. (The same would be equally true of a newspaper campaigning vigorously for joining the single currency.)

The *Sun*'s case is complicated by the knowledge that its proprietor, Rupert Murdoch, is known to be vehemently opposed to Britain's joining European Monetary Union and would not be unhappy that 10 million readers are being exposed to a barrage of opposing arguments. This is precisely the problem with disentangling the press's legitimate claim to be representing the people's interests with its slightly less legitimate role as representing a particular proprietorial or editorial view of the world. Nevertheless, on less controversial stories or political issues, it is possible sometimes to discern a genuine groundswell of popular discontent which is not created or fuelled by editorial self-interest. This raises an interesting question for the reporter's untainted role as tribune of the people: if we accept that it is sometimes possible to distil – without prejudice – a majoritarian view or even a consensus, how does a good political reporter go about assessing that consensus and passing it on?

Some light has been cast on this problem by Ralph Negrine in his analysis of how the press reported reactions in October 1992 to an announcement by British Coal that 31 out of 50 pits were to be closed, with the loss of 30,000 miners' jobs.[9] As Negrine reports, news of these closures had already been leaked and they were neither a secret nor unexpected. Nevertheless, the reaction in the popular press following the government's formal announcement – with headlines like the 'The Great Mine Disaster' in the Conservative-supporting *Daily Mail* – was an unpleasant surprise for the government. While early reports concentrated on what Negrine calls 'institutionalized' reactions (from trade unionists, MPs, etc.), the story as interpreted in virtually every newspaper developed into one of universal public outrage. They reported 'a nationwide wave of protests', a 'public furore', a 'tide of protest' and 'a popular backlash'. Negrine is almost certainly right to highlight the political context for these reports: a Prime Minister, John Major, who had lost credibility over Black Wednesday when Britain's entry into the Exchange Rate Mechanism failed spectacularly; and who was particularly despised within some sections of the Conservative press as being weak and indecisive (often being compared unfavourably to Margaret Thatcher, whom he had replaced).

Even within that context, however, political reporters clearly saw themselves as interpreters and communicators of the public mood rather than of their newspaper's agenda. And they felt able to pass accurate judgement on the state of public thinking by virtue of the sheer weight of communication directed at them, not just from professional lobby groups but from readers and other less committed sources. One reporter, asked how he came to his view of public thinking, said:

> 'Newspapers are at the receiving end of a tremendous amount of material. . . . It was one of the busiest times of my life. The phone never stopped ringing. Faxes came pouring in, and I had piles and piles of faxes from organizations, labour councils and so on. [It was] very, very unusual.'

The sheer scale of direct contact with newspapers was combined with a huge response being reported by some MPs, well beyond their normal expectations. Given the regular contact between political journalists and MPs, and the fact that many Conservative MPs were among the disenchanted, journalists were in this respect operating within an ideal-typical framework of the media's democratic function: not usurping MPs' role as elected tribunes of the people, but faithfully disseminating their views, which were in turn based on feedback from ordinary constituents. What was important in facilitating this process was that the 'backlash' crossed party lines. In the words of one reporter,

> 'We were taking our lead from what we were feeling was the view in the Commons. If all Tory MPs had just said "we don't care" and it had only been confined to Labour, then we would not have seen all these stories.'

On this evidence, we can conclude that under the right conditions it is *possible* (in that the mechanisms exist) for political journalists to act as the voice of the people. But the circumstances in which those conditions will all be satisfied are likely to be rare. First, it requires a political context in which the government (or a political individual) is seen as particularly vulnerable. Second, it requires a press – or at least a majority of the newspapers – which does not have a sustained pro-government agenda. It would have been hard, for example, to imagine the *Sun* during the premiership of Margaret Thatcher dedicating a completely blank front page to her Trade secretary with the explanation that 'It represents all that he understands about the worries and fears of the ordinary working people in depression-hit Britain. Nothing. Absolutely nothing.' None of the traditional Conservative-supporting papers – with the possible exception of the *Telegraph* – felt any such restraint under John Major.

Third, it requires dissent – or at the very least, disquiet – across normal party loyalties. Government measures are expected to be opposed by opposition MPs and by other bodies or organizations that will be adversely hit. In legislation affecting miners, journalists would expect the miners' union or the Trades Union Congress, or people associated with mining communities, to react with hostility. Things are different if that hostility is echoed from institutional sources normally expected to be government-friendly. Fourth, there need to be overt expressions of public anxiety. These can either be picked up by journalists themselves – through readers' letters and phone calls, by listening to phone-ins or observing demonstrations, or through their own family and friends – or can be conveyed to journalists via others who have themselves observed a widespread reaction, in particular MPs.

The press as information provider

At the information level, the ideal-type state of political reporting is relatively easy to define, if potentially rather dull in execution. It would involve publishing full accounts of current political debates, with impartial coverage of all sides of any arguments; saying who the proponents of different arguments are, and providing an honest assessment of the validity of those arguments; setting out the facts, including any research, statistics or background information which might be relevant to the issues under discussion; and describing the broader national and international context for the decisions to be taken. When, for example, new social security measures were being proposed to restrict payment to single parents, the information which ideally might have been available through the mass media would be the reasons that prompted such proposals; previous policy proposals in the same area; experience of other countries; figures on the numbers of people affected, their financial situations and the impact of the proposed measures; and the wider social and economic context, such as the impact on national expenditure.

It is important to distinguish between the provision of this kind of information during the normal political cycle, and the provision of information during election periods. Much research and writing has involved a critical analysis of the media's information role during elections, in which the ultimate aim is to ensure that electors are making informed electoral choices. This approach has been characterized by Golding, for example, as consumers in the political supermarket assessing their options before making their educated purchase at the check-out: 'The media play the part of consumer watch-dog, providing the means for the well-informed citizen to play his or her role to the full.'[10] The fact that in non-election periods there are no check-outs does not diminish the need for a citizenry to have access to a plurality of accurate, impartially presented information on important policy issues being discussed and implemented by elected representatives. Indeed, it is more likely to be outside the more intense scrutiny of election periods that the critical watchdog function of the media becomes even more vital as a means of holding governments to account.

What would be the criteria for measuring the 'success' of political journalism in information provision? Opinion polls conducted intermittently in the UK which ask about recognition of individual politicians suggest a fairly low level of cognitive knowledge. One US study, which asked some simple recognition questions in the 1970s, classified over two-thirds of voters as 'low knowledge' citizens, arguing as a result that journalists were consistently failing to hold the government to account and were avoiding more complex ideas or information.[11] More recent cross-cultural research looked at the contribution of television news to political knowledge across seven countries. By computing people's answers to five 'foreign affairs' questions and analysing their media usage, the study not only compared relative levels of knowledge but also tried to identify the main contributors. The authors concluded that 'in every country save the United Kingdom, regular reading of a newspaper made a statistically significant contribution to political knowledge'.[12] The average number of correct answers in the United States, the lowest of all seven countries apart from Spain, was directly attributed to American television and its lack of information about international politics.

A similar British study also seemed to demonstrate that exposure to television news was associated with relatively high levels of political knowledge, interest and understanding.[13] This study went further because it was attempting to test two contrasting theses about the role of the media in politics: the 'mobilization' theory, that greater penetration of news media into everyday life helps to mobilize people to greater interest and participation in the political system; and the 'video malaise' theory, that the media succeed only in alienating citizens, fostering an atmosphere of cynicism and distrust. By coming down firmly in favour of the former, at least in terms of television, it lends support to the view that 'good' political journalism can serve democracy. Given a sense that there is widespread and possibly increasing ignorance about some of the most important political issues which affect people's lives, the evidence suggests that modern political reporting has an important role to play in correcting that deficiency.

The press as enabler of opinion formation

This brings us to the third contribution that 'good' political journalism can make at the societal level: providing a forum for informed public opinion to evolve. The concept of 'rational-critical debate' owes much to the work of Jürgen Habermas, who took as his democratic model the coffee houses and salons of eighteenth-century Britain and France and believed that – ideally – a way should be found to 'make publicity a source of reasoned, progressive consensus formation'.[14] While the privilege of engaging in rational debate was limited in eighteenth-century Europe – much as in fifth-century BC Athens – to a privileged minority, it offers, in the words of James Curran, 'a powerful and arresting vision of the role of the media in a democratic society'. Curran describes the model of the public sphere as

> a neutral zone where access to relevant information affecting the public good is widely available, where discussion is free of domination and where all those participating in public debate do so on an equal basis. Within this public sphere, people collectively determine through the processes of rational argument the way in which they want to see society develop, and this shapes in turn the conduct of government policy.[15]

On one level it could be argued that the role of the political *journalist* (as opposed to the political media in general) is less central to the public sphere element of the democratic process. After all, the process of political reporting – gathering, filtering, interpreting and communicating information about the political world – is essentially a one-directional rather than a discursive process. Good reporters may be judged on the accuracy of their reports, on the quality of their contacts, on the persistence of their inquisitions when challenging authorized versions of events, or on their ability to tap into the channels of popular thinking. They cannot fairly be judged on whether they are prompting debate in the nation's pubs, offices, bus-stops, letters pages or phone-in programmes.

On the other hand, particularly in the broadcast media, the space that is given over for informed political debate, which can happen on screen (or on radio) and provoke further discussion among watching or listening audiences, is an important part of the journalistic process. Research has shown that programmes involving audience discussion, whether of an overtly political nature or the 'softer' issues often covered by morning talk shows, can play an important role in fostering a nation's political maturity. Decisions on whether to schedule such programmes, what issues to cover, and how to frame ensuing discussions are as much a part of the political journalistic fabric as lobby reports and evening news bulletins.[16] As increased commercial competition forces such programmes to move away from issues like 'Does the benefit system encourage single parenthood?' and towards the Jerry Springer model of 'Girls who run off with their best friend's husband', the public sphere model of broadcast journalism can fairly be said to be deteriorating. Again, however, we would emphasize that in its ideal-typical state, good journalism is quite capable of providing opportunities for rational-critical debate.

Effects at the individual level

The distinction between effects at the societal level and effects at the individual level is an important, if conceptual, one. Most standard media 'effects' studies in politics have been concerned with trying to establish a connection between exposure to the media and changes to individuals' political attitudes or behaviour. More significantly, they are usually tied to election campaigning, with increasingly sophisticated studies designed to identify and quantify which media can have an impact, how and on whom. A good recent example is a comprehensive effects study of the 1997 British general election, in which the authors start by distinguishing different types of media effect: 'on cognitive learning and political mobilization, on agenda-setting, on persuasion, and on voting behaviour'.[17] Although most attention tends to be focused on voting behaviour, issues of knowledge acquisition, attitude formation and stimulation to participate in the political arena are – as the authors point out – equally important in terms of assessing the contribution of political media to a nation's democratic culture. In a sophisticated series of linked studies, the authors found that those who were most attentive to the news media were both more politically knowledgeable and more likely to turn out to vote. As always, however, the direction of causation is much more difficult to resolve. Does exposure to politics through the media make people more politically aware and more willing to participate in the political process? Or are more politically aware people always more likely to pay particular attention to political news at election time?

The dilemmas surrounding experimental evidence on mobilization and cognitive effects are even more acute when it comes to voting patterns. At that point the questions cease to be an abstract (and perhaps slightly arcane) debate about the actual or potential contribution of mass media to democracy, and become a much more urgent debate about whether the media – in particular, individual channels or publications – actually have the power to change governments by influencing voting behaviour. This question has particularly exercised British scholars over the past fifteen years, and it is worth rehearsing briefly the nature of that debate – partly to illustrate how contrary and inconclusive evidence about effects can be, and partly to demonstrate that in our view the debate on media effects on voting has tended to conceal a far more significant influence: the impact on politicians and political parties rather than on voters themselves.

The debate began in earnest after the 1983 election, which saw the Conservatives, under Mrs Thatcher, romp home with a majority of 144. Following this dramatic triumph, the British General Election Study Campaign Panel researchers looked at the relationship between patterns of newspaper readership and electoral behaviour. They argued:

> The *Sun* may adopt strident rightwing views, but we see no evidence that this influenced its readers. The mere expression of political opinions, however forcefully put, appears to do little to sway people's votes. Our hypothesis is that information, not opinion, is needed in order to change voters' attitudes towards the parties.[18]

This was very much the standard view, as originally propounded by Butler and Stokes, who concluded in their study of the 1966 election that there was little evidence of electors switching their voting allegiances because of media exposure.[19] Martin Harrop looked at the 1983 election and, while agreeing with the broad thrust of the prevailing consensus, did observe that where there was no established political allegiance there could be a modest press impact on voting behaviour.[20]

However, in the following election in 1987, William Miller, using data from the British General Election Study, claimed to have discerned a significant pro-Conservative 'effect' that could be traced back to the influence of the tabloids. His research found that Labour identifiers who read a right-wing paper were 6 per cent more favourable to Margaret Thatcher and 6 per cent less favourable to Neil Kinnock than Labour identifiers who did not. Moreover, in the twelve months leading up to the election, the Conservative lead over Labour increased by 34 per cent among the pro-Tory *Sun* and *Daily Star* readers but by a mere 2 per cent among the pro-Labour *Mirror* readers: 'the tabloids were particularly good at influencing their reader's voting preferences'.[21]

This view appeared to be given substantial credence by events leading up to the 1992 general election. With the demise of Margaret Thatcher and the country in the grip of a recession, most commentators (and many opinion polls) put the Labour Party ahead in a closely fought context. One of the features of the campaign was a series of ferociously bitter attacks on the Labour leader, Neil Kinnock, in the newspapers most associated with the right, in particular the *Daily Mail* and the *Sun*. When the Conservatives won with a comparatively comfortable majority of 21, both scholars and politicians started to point accusing fingers at the right-wing press – in particular, given its readership of 10 million, the *Sun*.

It was frequently noted that working-class voters in the South had swung sharply to the Conservatives in the last few days of the campaign, and that the *Sun* sold strongly in the region. Indeed, Basildon, a new town east of London and an important symbolic Conservative success on election night, had the highest proportion of *Sun* readers in the country. Martin Linton, a former *Guardian* journalist turned Labour MP, believed that the *Sun*'s influence was decisive in securing a fourth term for the Conservatives and undertook a research project specifically designed to address that question. By tracking opinion poll movements among *Sun* readers, he claimed to demonstrate that in the months leading up to the election, the increase in Conservative Party support was greater among *Sun* readers than for any other group of newspaper readers.[22]

The problem with Linton's case was that, as ever, he appeared to establish correlation but not causation. His conclusions have been challenged by a number of scholars from a variety of perspectives. Harrop and Scammell have argued, first, that the tabloid press was at least as partisan, if not more so, in the 1983 and 1987 campaigns, neither of which saw a similar late anti-Labour swing. Second, the late swing in 1992 was not confined to readers of anti-Tory papers; readers of the non-aligned *Independent* and readers of the staunchly pro-Labour *Daily Mirror* swung by almost as large a percentage away from Labour in the final days of the campaign as did *Sun readers. The Express* and *Mail* also provided a very partisan – if less strident – coverage in favour of the Tories, but their readership was less moved.[23] Ivor Crewe has calculated that the impact of the *Sun*'s campaigning was worth no more than six highly marginal seats at most, all in areas of high *Sun* popularity.[24]

John Curtice has also challenged the theory that the tabloid press is a major determinant of changes in voting behaviour, concentrating in particular on the problem of proving causation:

> One of the biggest difficulties in undertaking research on the influence of the media is disentangling cause and effect. It is relatively easy to demonstrate that those people who read, say, a pro-Conservative newspaper, are more likely to vote Conservative. But we cannot tell how far this arises because people choose which newspaper to read because of its politics and how far it is the result of the influence a newspaper has on its readers.[25]

And newspaper readership is not constant. In spring 1995, when the

British General Election Study covering the 1992 election was completed, only 69 per cent had the same newspaper-reading habits as they had had at the time of the election. Changes can reflect people moving towards a newspaper because they like what it is saying rather than the newspapers' existing readers being influenced by the paper. Curtice claims that data from the 1987-92 British General Election Study Campaign Panel indicates that there is no strong evidence that 'those reading a Conservative-inclined newspaper swung to the Conservatives more strongly than any other group did during the course of the campaign'. In support of this argument Curtice looked to the data from the Panel study gathered in 1995. This was at a time when Conservative support in the press was fracturing – the *Daily Express* and the *Daily Telegraph* staying loyal but the *Sun*, the *Daily Star*, the *Daily Mail* and *The Times* all expressing grave doubts about John Major's government. If a newspaper effects model were operating, he would have expected to find support for the Conservatives draining away more quickly among readers of this latter group of newspapers; but no such effect was identifiable.

Despite the generally unconvinced state of the academic community about the power of the press, it was perhaps predictable when Labour swept to power in 1997 that fingers should point once more at the astonishing turnaround in press partisanship. Ten years earlier, in the 1987 election, the Conservatives were able to rely on every national newspaper bar the *Daily Mirror* and the *Guardian* for support. By 1997 only the *Daily Telegraph* and *Daily Express* remained completely loyal to the Tory cause (even the *Mail* had become equivocal), and by the following year the *Express* had effectively jumped ship. Although this was an astonishing turnaround in press support, it coincided with a period when the Labour Party had enjoyed consistent and record-breaking support in opinion polls and at the ballot box. Probably the most dramatic, and certainly the most publicized, of those conversions was that of the *Sun* to the Labour cause on the opening day of the 1997 election campaign. Making the link was for many people irresistible. As Scammell and Harrop have written, 'Labour has never had such a favourable press at a general election, nor has it ever achieved such a stunning majority in terms of seats. It is tempting to imagine that these two facts must be linked somehow.'[26]

Many have tried to make that connection, but the only authoritative study to date has come to the same negative conclusions as Curtice and others following the 1992 election. Summarizing the results of their analysis of the British General Election Study Campaign data, Norris *et al.* concluded:

> The 1997 election provided a clear opportunity for the power of the press, and of Britain's top-selling newspaper in particular, to reveal itself. In practice . . . it still tended to prefer to remain in hiding. The *Sun*'s conversion did not evidently bring the Labour Party new recruits. Equally Labour's new recruits did not prove particularly keen to switch to the *Sun*. At best we have found, in line with our previous research, that newspapers have but a limited influence on the voting behaviour of their readers.[27]

The 'real' media effect: on politicians rather than voters

It is therefore tempting to conclude that the influence of the press on voters is illusory rather than real and leave the matter there. In fact, perhaps the most important consequence of this debate is the conviction among politicians – and many journalists – that the press *does* change people's minds. Ever since the advent of Margaret Thatcher to the Conservative Party leadership in 1975, the fervent and unstinting support of the *Sun* was perceived as one of the most powerful weapons in the Conservative Party's armoury. It did not matter that the perception was ill-founded, particularly since it was rein-forced in the aftermath of the Conservative Party's unexpected triumph in the 1992 election by some of the key players of the time. Lord McAlpine, a former party treasurer, expressed the gratitude of many Tories for the role played by the tabloids in their victory: 'The heroes of this campaign were Sir David English [editor of the *Daily Mail*], Sir Nicholas Lloyd [editor of the *Daily Express*], Kelvin McKenzie [editor of the *Sun*] and the other editors of the grander Tory press.'[28] Labour was quick to endorse this judgement. The defeated Labour leader, Neil Kinnock, said, 'Never in the past nine elections have they [the Conservative press] come out so strongly in favour of the Conservatives. Never has their attack on the Labour party been so compre-hensive. This was how the election was won.'[29] It is therefore hardly surprising that the unambiguous view within the Labour Party after 1992 was that support of more newspapers, and in particular the *Sun*, was going to be crucial to winning an election. On hearing the news, at the start of the 1997 campaign, that the *Sun* was backing Labour, a senior member of Labour's team said: 'That's it. We can't be beaten now.'[30] Following Labour's victory in 1997, Labour leader and newly anointed Prime Minister Tony Blair sent a handwritten message to the editor of the *Sun* in which he thanked the paper for its 'magnificent support' and said it 'really did make the difference'.[31]

There is no question that on being elected leader of the Labour Party, Tony Blair went out of his way to court Rupert Murdoch, the *Sun*'s proprietor. His trip to the Hayman Islands in 1995 to address senior executives of News Corporation was much publicized and much speculated upon, and there have certainly been suggestions that certain policy shifts could be attributed to Blair's determination to get Murdoch onside. As the General Election of 1997 approached, the Labour Party's position on the Single European Cur-rency – to which the *Sun* and its proprietor remain implacably opposed – appeared to harden considerably. Three years later, the series of damaging leaks which emerged from inside the Prime Minister's office in the summer of 2000 quickly became a graphic and notorious illustration of the way in which modern party leaders govern with both eyes closely trained on the media. One, written by the Prime Minister himself two months before it was leaked, complained of 'a sense that the Government . . . are somehow out of touch with gut British instincts'. He talked about the need for a strategy to combat perceptions of weakness, and focused on five specific areas: asylum, crime, defence, the family, and the need to review sentencing law in the light of a recent case where a man who had killed an intruder was convicted of murder and given a mandatory life sentence as a result. On the very day the Prime Minister had written that memo – 29 April – a *Daily Mail* editorial had railed against a 'liberal establishment' and specifically mentioned four of the five areas identified in Blair's note as requiring attention.[32]

A second memo, written a few days later by Blair's strategist Philip Gould, was almost apocalyptic in its predictions that Labour's huge majority was in danger at the next election and warned that 'We quickly seem to have grown out of touch.' It concluded, 'We need to be far simpler and more professional. We need to get back in touch. We need to reinvent the New Labour brand.'[33] Such marketing-speak, though much derided by most of Blair's cabinet, had been regarded as hugely influential in Labour's election success. What emerged from this leaked memo, however, was the way in which the government's perception was dominating the prime ministerial agenda, and what constituted the most influential filters of that perception for Downing Street's inner core. This world of mirrors within mirrors was brilliantly exposed by Hugo Young's verdict in the *Guardian* on Gould's influence:

> In both his book and his memos, appearance is what dominates. The politics of perception is all. What people think is what matters. It should be your guide, both on what to do and on whether your actions are effective. In Gould's world, perception, far from being at odds with reality, *is* reality. And that is exactly Labour's problem. Its substance is not apparent. Its manipulation is too obvious. . . . Though the *Daily Mail* isn't mentioned in these memos, it is the fountain-head of wisdom Blair must tap into, notwithstanding the fact, which Gould well knows, that only 13% of its readers contributed their vote to the Labour landslide.[34]

In terms of political influence, then, the real significance is not the impact exerted by the media on public opinion, but the impact exerted by the perceived effect of the media on public opinion by an almost obsessive political class. That the press can change the course of governments is at best unproven and at worst nonsense. That politicians are irredeemably convinced that the press can change governments means that they are almost obsessed by the nature of political reporting in those media and prepared to go to many lengths – some would say any lengths – to ensure that such coverage is favourable. The nature of political reporting is therefore crucial, almost *regardless* of its impact on electors.

Notes

1. James S. Fishkin (1995) *The Voice of the People: Public Opinion and Democracy*, p. 76. New Haven: Yale University Press.
2. Andrew Adonis and Geoff Mulgan (1994) 'Back to Greece: the scope for direct democracy', *Demos*, no. 3, pp. 2–9.
3. Quoted in Robert Tyrrell and David Goodhart (1998) 'Opinion poll democracy', *Prospect*, October, pp. 50–4.
4. Roza Tsagarousianou (1998) 'Electronic democracy and the public sphere', in Roza Tsagarousianou, Damian Tambini and Cathy Bryan (eds) *Cyberdemocracy: Technology, Cities and Civic Networks*, p. 170. London: Routledge.

5. Roy Hattersley (1996) 'The unholy alliance: the relationship between Members of Parliament and the press'. James Cameron Memorial Lecture, 23 April. London: City University.

6. Fishkin, *op. cit.*, p. 23.

7. Steven Barnett and Katarina Thomson (1996) 'Portraying sex: the limits of tolerance', in Roger Jowell, John Curtice, Alison Park, Lindsay Brook and Katarina Thomson (eds) *British Social Attitudes, the 13th Report*, p. 39. Aldershot: Dartmouth Press.

8. Interview, December 1998.

9. Ralph Negrine (1996) *The Communication of Politics*, pp. 112–26. London: Sage.

10. Peter Golding (1990) 'Political communication and citizenship: the media and democracy in an inegalitarian social order', in Marjorie Ferguson (ed.) *Public Communication: The New Imperatives*, p. 84. London: Sage.

11. Robert M. Entman (1989) *Democracy without Citizens: Media and the Decay of American Politics*. Oxford: Oxford University Press.

12. Michael Dimock and Samuel Popkin (1997) 'Political knowledge in comparative perspective', in Shanto Iyengar and Richard Reeves (eds) *Do the Media Govern?*, p. 218. London: Sage.

13. Kenneth Newton (1997), 'Politics and the news media: mobilisation or videomalaise?', in Roger Jowell, John Curtice, Alison Park, Lindsay Brooke, Katarina Thomson and Caroline Bryson (eds) *British Social Attitudes, the 14th Report*. Aldershot: Ashgate Publishing.

14. Craig Calhoun (1992) Introduction to *Habermas and the Public Sphere*. Cambridge, Mass.: MIT Press.

15. James Curran (1996) 'Mass media and democracy revisited', in James Curran and Michael Gurevitch (eds) *Mass Media and Society*, 2nd edition, p. 82. London: Arnold.

16. See, for example, Sonia Livingstone and Peter Lunt (1994) *Talk on Television*. London: Routledge. In their analysis of television viewers' reactions to talk shows, they argue that 'viewers are operating with Habermasian ideals, expecting to hear a rational discussion leading to a critical consensus' (p. 160).

17. Pippa Norris, John Curtice, David Sanders, Margaret Scammell and Holli Semetks (1999) *On Message: Communicating the Campaign*, p. 13. London: Sage.

18. Anthony Heath, Roger Jowell and John Curtice (1985) *How Britain Votes*, p. 149. Oxford: Pergamon Press.

19. David Butler and Donald Stokes (1969) *Political Change in Britain*. London: Macmillan.

20. Martin Harrop (1986) 'Press coverage of post-war British elections', in Ivor Crewe and Martin Harrop (eds) *Political Communications: The British General Election Campaign of 1983*. Cambridge: Cambridge University Press.

21. William Miller (1990) *Media and Voters: The Audience, Content and Influence of Press and Television in the 1987 General Election*, p. 199. Oxford: Clarendon Press.

22. Martin Linton (1996) 'Maybe the *Sun* won it after all', *British Journalism Review*, vol. 7, no. 2, pp. 20–6. This article was based on a *Guardian* lecture by Linton, and the title was based on the *Sun* headline the day after the election: 'It Was the Sun Wot Won It'.

23. Margaret Scammell and Martin Harrop (1992) 'A tabloid war', in David Butler and Denis Kavanagh (eds) *The British General Election of 1992*, pp. 180–210. Basingstoke: Macmillan.

24. Ivor Crewe (1992) 'Why did Labour lose (yet) again?', *Politics Review*, vol. 2, no. 1, September, pp. 2–11.

25. John Curtice (1996) 'Is the *Sun* shining on Tony Blair?'. Paper delivered to the Annual Meeting of the American Political Sciences Association (British Politics Group) at the San Francisco Hilton, 29 August – 1 September.

26. Scammell and Harrop, *op. cit.*, p. 183.

27. Norris *et al.*, *op. cit.*, p. 168.

28. Quoted in Scammell and Harrop, *op. cit.*, p. 208.

29. *Ibid.*

30. Private conversation.

31. Roy Greenslade (1997) 'Nice One Sun, says Tony', *Guardian*, 19 May, section 2, p. xx.

32. The full text of the memo was published in several papers, although the original leak was to

the two daily Murdoch papers, the *Sun* and *The Times*. See *Daily Telegraph*, 18 July 2000, p. 4; *Guardian*, 18 July 2000, pp. 4–5; and *Daily Mail*, 18 July 2000, pp. 4–5, which also published its own original editorial.

33. Published in full in the *Sun*, 19 July 2000, pp. 2–3.

34. Hugo Young (2000) 'The leaks show whose heads must roll. That of Gould', *Guardian*, 20 July 2000, p. 18.

CHAPTER THREE

The contours of political coverage: who does what in political journalism[1]

There never was a 'golden age' of political communications – a time when journalists were able to report everything happening in government and the parties and politicians were satisfied that their actions and views were being fairly represented. Such a situation is both mythical and, probably, undesirable. For while a degree of co-operation is required between the media and politicians, this should always be leavened by a healthy dose of tension: the political commentator Peter Kellner has used the phrase 'collusive conflict' to describe this relationship. However, whether it be conversations in the press gallery bar or memoirs by politicians or journalists, the constant refrain is always of how much better political journalism used to be. John Cole, who between 1981 and 1992 was the BBC's Political Editor, after more than forty years of political reporting is gloomy: 'Politicians and the media seemed to be on a course of mutual injury if not destruction. In the words of matrimonial law here was a relationship in danger of having irretrievably broken down.'[2]

The memoirs of political reporters from an earlier time give a flavour of a more deferential era at Westminster. E. Clepham Palmer, who sat in the press gallery for the *News Chronicle* in the inter-war period, has written:

> As a whole, Parliament is a little self-contained world with an *esprit de corps* of its own. Ministers, backbenchers, officials, journalists, attendants, police and the staff generally all contribute to the spirit of the place. There could hardly be a pleasanter or more fascinating little world to work in.[3]

And Alan Pitt Robbins, *The Times*'s Parliamentary Correspondent, speaking in 1929, saw a role for journalists as almost constitutionally defined: 'I like to regard the Lobby correspondent as the "liaison officer" between Parliament and the public.'[4] Sir Alexander Mackintosh, a regional parliamentary correspondent between 1881 and 1940, believed that this liaison role was carried out to the evident satisfaction of the journalists' political masters: 'The value of their [the political correspondents'] liaison work as between Government and public is more frankly appreciated and is well understood by the leading statesmen.'[5] But it is to veteran political correspondent James Margach, who reported on a dozen prime ministers from Stanley Baldwin in the 1920s to James Callaghan in the 1970s, that one turns for a more robust interpretation of the relationship between journalists and politicians:

As Whitehall has accumulated more and more power from Westminster, the techniques of news-management and centralised control have become more complete while secrecy is more widespread and ruthlessly organised, sustaining the mystique of power which in turn sustains all Prime Ministers.[6]

However, one of the major changes that has emerged in media coverage of politics over the past two decades has been the enlargement of the number of journalists actually involved in political reporting. This enlargement has taken place as political reporting has spread from the lobby (discussed below), which for many years exercised a virtual monopoly of the trade, to a whole range of other areas of journalistic enterprise.

The term 'political journalist' is in fact a very broad-brush description of all those whose work involves writing and broadcasting about politics. For the purposes of analysing the political news production process it is important to have a clear understanding of the differences between parliamentary reporters, political correspondents, political columnists and so forth.

The different guises of a political journalist

The very first political reporters were in fact parliamentary reporters – journalists whose sole function was to sit in the press gallery of the House of Commons recording and reporting the debates. Their activities have declined dramatically. Nowadays the vast majority of this reporting is undertaken by specialist reporters working for Hansard, the official publication of the House (named after the first printer-publisher of parliamentary debates). In addition, the national news agency, the Press Association, a company jointly owned by the main regional newspapers, has a team of gallery reporters who, unlike the Hansard reporters, do not transcribe every word uttered in the chamber but nonetheless supply the media with a substantial and rapid reporting service. The amount of parliamentary reporting to be found in the national press has been in steady decline. Indeed, during the last decade of the twentieth century no national newspaper carried parliamentary reports on a daily basis. However, since 2000 the four broadsheets – *The Times*, *Guardian*, *Independent* and *Daily Telegraph* – have returned to the practice of carrying a daily page of reports from Parliament. There is an arguable case that this change was the result of a series of interventions from politicians and journalists.

Nicholas Watt, now of the *Guardian*, observed this decline in parliamentary reporting over the past decade:

'[A]s recently as ten years ago every national newspaper would have had staff permanently in the press gallery taking a full note, because they would have had a page or two pages of verbatim reporting. Very, very straight reporting, "The Secretary of State for Scotland said yesterday . . ." That has all changed. The papers have taken away their traditional gallery reporting; they still have politics pages, but they want news stories – sometimes they come from the chamber, sometimes from elsewhere, sometimes [they are] an amalgamation of what happened in the chamber or in a select committee or in a briefing. That means you have far less [*sic*] reporters actually sitting in the press gallery.'[7]

This decline in parliamentary reporting has been tracked by *Guardian* journalist David McKie, who compared the amount of parliamentary, as opposed to political, coverage that four broadsheet newspapers – *The Times*, the *Daily Telegraph*, the *Guardian* and the *Financial Times* – carried in 1996 and 1946.[8] His figures demonstrated that in the past fifty years the amount of column inches devoted to Parliament had dropped from a total of 11,443 in an average week in 1946 to just 3,222 in 1996 – a fall of over 70 per cent. And this despite the increased number of pages available to the 1996 broadsheets. Jack Straw, a senior Labour government minister, waged a campaign against this reduction in the amount of reporting of Parliament now carried by the national press. Straw adduced four reasons for the decline:

- the televising of Parliament, which led to television displacing newspapers as the most immediate source of parliamentary news;
- a generational change among broadsheet editors, who came to see parliamentary debates as 'boring';
- a consequential change in the behaviour of MPs, who, seeing the trend, used press releases and interviews as a more effective way of engaging in the national debate; and
- the large Conservative majorities of the 1980s, which meant that the government was always assured of winning parliamentary votes.[9]

An additional factor that Jack Straw failed to mention lay in the rise of the select committees. The current structure of the committees was established in 1980 but it was only with the introduction of televised hearings in 1989 that their public profile really began to take shape. Four years after televising began, the authors undertook research on the effects of televising committees and concluded that their influence was growing:

> Television is acting as a catalyst to transform the nature and role of select committees from a monitoring system to a system of influence through accountability, efficiency and education. It may be that constitutionally there is little in common with the American model of congressional committees. But the publicity effects will not be dissimilar. And it may not be long before real power will finally accrue via the lever of television's publicity.[10]

The subsequent seven years have demonstrated a notable growth in the power and influence of select committees and a concurrent fall in the influence of the main chamber. The media have failed to respond fully to this change, perceiving the decline in importance of the chamber and therefore reducing coverage but failing to respond to the rise in the influence of the committees. The result has been an overall decline in the actual reporting of Parliament.

Politicians have perceived that making a speech in the chamber is not an effective way of getting their messages across to the public. Indeed, one backbench MP has joked, during a discussion about freedom of information, that the best way for the government to keep its secrets, while at the same time paying 'lip-service' to its commitment to freedom of information, was for a minister to make a speech on the floor of the House – no one would notice, but the government could always later claim that the issue had been subjected to public discussion.[11] As a result of this decline, many individual politicians have become virtually one-person media operations. They flood the broadcasters and press with their news releases, make themselves available for interview at all hours of the day and night, and tip off friendly journalists with stories. This activity is most pronounced at the regional level. Ken Livingstone, a leader of the Greater London Council in the 1980s, compared his experience then and in 1999 when he was starting his campaign to be nominated as Labour's candidate for Mayor of London:

> Twenty years ago you would spend most of the day being grilled by newspaper journalists and then rattle off four quick interviews, one each for BBC and ITV, radio and TV. Nowadays, you aim to try to cover all journalists at one half-hour press conference and spend the rest of the day repeating the same basic message to what seem like dozens of separate radio and television programmes.[12]

Backbench MPs, as Ken Livingstone was, very soon learn that the national media have very little interest in them – unless of course they are in the process of rebelling against their own party's leadership. However, their regional media – the local and regional press, but particularly the BBC's local radio stations – have a much greater appetite for their activities. Hence, the relationship between regional journalists and MPs in their patch can be much more intense. Indeed, as and when local MPs move up the ministerial ladder, and journalists move from regional to national media, these relationships can come to play a very significant role; trust built up over the years can provide the journalist with some excellent news leads.[13]

The decline in interest in the chamber has led to an increase in the visibility of political correspondents – the so-called 'lobby' (also known as lobby correspondents) – at the expense of the now almost defunct breed of parliamentary reporters. The role of lobby correspondents is discussed in more detail below, but the broad category can be subdivided into three distinct sub-species. At the top of the political food chain is the *political editor* – a senior figure with direct lines to his own editor, to Downing Street and to the Leader of the Opposition's office. Nicholas Watt, now of the *Guardian* but formerly of *The Times*, described how this 'pecking order' can be observed on the pages of some particular newspapers:

> 'Everyone jokes about it, how the *Times* political editor has his little slot reserved for him on the front page where his byline goes every day. And if you look at the *The Times* you'll see that every single day his name's there, on the second story you'll find the number two's name on it.'[14]

The 'number two' (of whom there may be more than one) is generally known as the *political correspondent*, and will handle the majority of the stories that are regarded as significant. (In some organizations political correspondents are given the accolade of chief political correspondent in order to distinguish them from their colleagues.) Finally, at the bottom – often referred to as 'pond life' – are the political reporters, sometimes bylined simply as 'political staff' (although such a byline is also used to disguise the fact that a story has been culled from the wires of the Press Association news agency).

If the decline in parliamentary reporting has not led to any concomitant increase in political reporting, it certainly has coincided over the past few years with a marked increase in newspaper space devoted to star-name political columnists. Names like Donald Macintyre on the *Independent*, Hugo Young on the *Guardian* and Peter Riddell on *The Times* have a status as high as, if not higher than, that of political editors. Many columnists are former lobby correspondents themselves, and some still retain their lobby cards. However, their work differs significantly from that of their colleagues in the lobby because their job is not to report on the day's political news or even to break 'exclusives'. Their roles can best be described as policy, sometimes personality, analysis. They talk to politicians and observe them in action, but they also talk with and participate in the so-called 'policy community' – attend conferences and seminars, write for think tanks, mix with academics, and so on.

The growth of political columnists has caused MPs some concerns because, given the columnists' lack of dependence on a daily news flow, they are less susceptible to the kinds of pressures that politicians and their advisers can bring to bear on lobby correspondents. However, even more than the political columnist, the breed of political journalist that gives politicians most cause for concern is the parliamentary sketchwriter – a trade that has boomed with the decline of parliamentary reporting. On an average slow news day in the House of Commons the benches of the press gallery will be virtually deserted but for the Hansard note-takers, the ever-present Press Association reporter and the parliamentary sketchwriters. They usually occupy the front benches of the Gallery, and on most days can be seen leaning over the balcony trying to catch an MP dozing, reading a copy of the *Sun* or simply wearing a pair of outlandish braces. They wait for the inappropriate phrase or gesture, the unexpected outburst or the quirky moment that will provide them with the material for their daily column. Sketchwriters need to be witty and trenchant, and, most worryingly for MPs, they have a self-declared mission to mock. Given the decline in straightforward reporting of Parliament, MPs are particularly concerned that these sketches are now virtually the only perspective on the conduct of MPs to be found in the press on a daily basis.

Sketchwriting is a well-established Westminster trade. A relatively new aspect of political reporting, however, is the rise of the so-called Whitehall or Westminster correspondents.[15] They cover what is cumbersomely known as the machinery of government, the civil service, quangos and so on. The first such reporter was Anthony Howard, who in 1965 was appointed the *Sunday Times*'s Whitehall Correspondent. It was an appointment that so enraged the then Prime Minister, Harold Wilson, that he instructed his cabinet colleagues to have no dealings with Howard – a move that ensured that Howard received a steady stream of calls from disaffected members of the cabinet.[16] The role of these 'governance' correspondents in exposing government incompetence, corruption and plain misguided policies has been much enhanced by the higher profile and greater level of activity of the House of Commons Public Accounts Committee and the agency that services it, the National Audit Office. Whitehall reporters, the Public Accounts Committee (PAC) and the National Audit Office exist side by side in a slightly ambiguous relationship. All three groupings are seeking to reveal scandals and maladministration; the only difference is one of timescale. The journalist wants to break the story before its official publication, and that means even before the advanced copies of the document have been delivered to members of the lobby. The PAC and the Audit Office, on the other hand, want to bathe in the glory of their own publicity, undistracted by premature leaks in the media. This creates an odd sort of relationship for this breed of journalist. On the one hand they need to have good relations with members of the PAC and the Audit Office, for these are clearly important sources of information, but on the other hand they are also competitors.

It would be mistaken to believe that only reporters based in and around Westminster are involved in political coverage. For in the past few years there has been a significant growth in the range and number of specialist correspondents on newspapers, television and the radio. For some time there have been diplomatic, industrial and defence correspondents. More recently, there has grown a whole plethora of specialist journalists covering education, home affairs, health, social services, transport, environment, consumer affairs, media and sport. This has resulted in a change of tactics by government. In general, departments now prefer to deal with what they tend to regard as their 'own' specialist reporters. This is because press officers believe that these journalists understand the issues, are usually more 'sympathetic' and are more amenable to pressure. Any specialist correspondent seen to be 'difficult' will find his or her ability to gain access to 'off the record' briefings that much more difficult to obtain. As a result, more and more news is pre-released to specialist correspondents before it finds its way to the lobby. Press officers in Whitehall have very few dealings with the Westminster political correspondents, as opposed to their almost daily contact with their relevant specialist reporters.

This rise in specialist correspondents has taken place both in the press and in broadcasting, but television and radio also require a whole range of specialists of their own to enable them to function effectively in the political arena. For broadcast journalists are involved in more than just gathering and disseminating information; they are also involved in producing radio and television programmes. Once a newspaper journalist has obtained the relevant information, it is then a relatively simple matter to write up the story for publication. For radio and television journalists, obtaining the information is only the start of the process. Behind the front-line troops whose faces are seen and voices heard, there stands a veritable army of journalists all toiling to produce the finished product.

At a junior level there are researchers who undertake the basic research and 'phone bashing'[17] – an essential part of the production process. These researchers do not just assist in information-gathering; more crucially, they are 'seeking out the bodies' – looking for politicians who are prepared to say into a microphone or camera what their colleagues have been whispering into the ear of the lobby correspondent.

Next in the chain of production are the political writers and producers who are responsible for assembling the material – parliamentary or other actuality material – as well as carrying out some of the interviews which go to make up the final news packages that are presented by the political correspondents.

There are also the programme presenters – political specialists themselves, whose work is confined to the television and radio studios and hence need the support of producers and researchers. And finally there are political programme editors, who take the crucial editorial decisions based on the advice they are receiving from their teams of political correspondents and producers. Thus in broadcasting much of the most significant decision-taking is undertaken by broadcast journalists who have little direct contact with the raw material: the politicians. Certainly lunches are arranged and receptions held where these behind-the-scenes broadcasters can get to know the politicians a little better; but this is no substitute for the day-to-day contact that journalists working in the lobby are able to maintain. Hence, despite the great complexity of broadcast journalism, the system of restricted parliamentary access which the lobby symbolizes means that significant power still lies in the hands of the political correspondents and their unattributable sources.

The lobby

Some three years ago there occurred a landmark day in British political reporting. On 27 November 1997 the new Labour government formally announced that the twice-daily press briefing from the Prime Minister's press secretary to the lobby was now to be 'on the record'. Until then, such meetings never officially took place; these briefings were always held on a non-attributable basis. This required the deployment of well-worn phrases such as 'sources close to the Prime Minister' and 'a senior Downing Street source' which enabled the Prime Minister to distance him- or herself from the original remarks if necessary. And Downing Street's *amour-propre* was pro-tected by the lobby itself; according to their own rules, members are (or were) supposed to deny that the meetings had even taken place.[18]

The lobby came into existence in 1884. Until that time members of the public had been free to mingle with MPs in the members' lobby outside the chamber of the House of Commons. However, following a series of Irish bomb attacks the public were banned from the lobby. In order to enable journalists to have continued access to politicians, the Serjeant-at-Arms, the official responsible for security at Westminster, discreetly set up a list of accredited correspondents. Thus was born the lobby. Over the years, the lobby – now almost 200 strong – was subjected to increasing criticism as it came to be seen almost as an additional arm of the government's information machine because it allowed government spokesmen to speak 'off the record'. As Cockerell *et al.* put it:

> It is this rule of non-attribution which is the Lobby's most distinctive characteristic, and coupled with the credulity of many of its members it has turned the Lobby into the Prime Minister's most useful tool for the political management of the news.[19]

For a period in the 1980s the *Independent*, the *Guardian* and the *Scotsman* newspapers boycotted the lobby briefings. This boycott had been occasioned by one particular Downing Street Press Secretary – Bernard, now Sir Bernard, Ingham – who served Margaret Thatcher between 1979 and 1990. He was ruthless in using the unattributable nature of the briefings to denigrate politicians who were out of favour with the Prime Minister and to boost those whose star was in the ascendant. He has admitted that great tension existed between Downing Street and the lobby, and illustrated this tension with reference to his own role in the events in Paris, prior to Margaret Thatcher's resignation in 1990, when he was seen to step out of his government role and adopt a more overtly political one. He writes:

> This celebrated cameo of government–press relations has many lessons, not the least of which is the impossibility of satisfying British journalists. They subsequently charged me with anything from 'bullying' to 'activities unbecoming of a civil servant', even though I was serving their purposes.[20]

With Margaret Thatcher's fall from power and Ingham's departure from Downing Street, the lobby boycotters returned to the fold, but criticism of the lobby has continued. BBC Political Correspondent Nicholas Jones has, in a series of books, been mounting the case for the twice-daily briefings to be broadcast live on television and radio. But many of the journalists who work in the lobby are stout defenders of the system. David Wastell, the Political Editor of the *Sunday Telegraph*, believes that the lobby functions like any other group of journalists working in close proximity:

> 'The mystique of the lobby as an organization that receives secret briefings and all that sort of thing is over-hyped in my view. A lot of nonsense gets written about it. . . . It's just a lot of journalists talking to a lot of people all in the same place, all at the same time . . . when I first joined the lobby, I was told by someone who had been here a long time that you weren't ever allowed to put anything that was said in a briefing in direct quotes, and frankly people were already ignoring it and I ignored it. But I wouldn't say "Bernard Ingham said", I would say "a senior Whitehall source" – everyone knew what the code was. The code has been simplified now, but there is still a code. Isn't there in all journalism? If you're in business journalism and you talk to the managing director at some company, then you will say "senior sources at company X", it's just the same thing.'[21]

The Political Editor of the *Sunday Telegraph* would be seen as very much part of the lobby 'establishment'. Newcomers, particularly those working for news organizations that would not be seen as 'mainstream', see things very differently. Chris Wickham is the first correspondent from the American–owned Dow Jones news agency, which specializes in economic stories. To someone looking upwards from the bottom of the pile, the lobby looked very different:

> 'I'd say that working in the lobby has been the most peculiar experience I've had in journalism so far . . . to a large extent the lobby and the structure of the lobby reflect in a sense the structure and the atmosphere of Parliament itself. It's an extremely clubby institution . . . to a large extent it serves the status quo in whatever form you want to interpret that . . . the lobby itself has its own hierarchy where the political editors of certain British newspapers are at the top of that hierarchy.'[22]

The briefings take place at 11 a.m. in 10 Downing Street and at 4 p.m. at the House of Commons, and they are now available in an attenuated form on the Downing Street website. Although the lobby consists of around 200 correspondents, unless there is a major story running, barely one in ten attend the briefings. From 10.45 onwards groups of journalists can be seen shuffling between Parliament and Downing Street, making their way to the morning lobby briefings, which take place in a specially built conference room in the basement of 10 Downing Street. A few minutes later the entourage of officials sweeps in, usually led by the Prime Minister's Press Secretary or his deputy. They are accompanied by four or five other press officers, either from Downing Street or from departments that are likely to feature in that day's news agenda. The briefing begins with the Press Secretary drawing attention to matters about which most news organizations are already aware such as government press notices and forthcoming press conferences.

He then moves into what can appear rather tedious parliamentary technicalities, but for broadcasters involved in live political programming and for evening newspaper correspondents, these represent vital information. For the Press Secretary draws attention to one or two of the many so-called 'written answers' by ministers which will be published in the House later that day. These are in effect planted questions which ministers use as means of getting information into the public domain without having to navigate the perils and pitfalls of being cross-questioned by MPs or journalists. In addition, Ministerial Statements, or so-called Private Notice Questions upcoming later in the day, are also signalled. The Press Secretary then recounts the Prime Minister's plans for the day, which do not usually go much beyond 'meetings with ministerial colleagues and others'. He then invites questions.

The pecking order for questions so rigorously established during election press conferences (that is, taking initial questions from the broadcasters, who need to be seen and heard live on air) is not quite so rigorously followed at the daily briefings (although the broadcasters, presumably by force of habit, still position themselves at the front). This question-and-answer session can be desultory, abrasive and occasionally amusing. The Press Secretary is asked about the Prime Minister's views on various stories that have cropped up, either in the morning newspapers or on the morning's radio and television (BBC Radio's *Today* programme being a primary source). Equally, he might be invited to speculate on government action about some other unfolding or anticipated event. There is a little sparring, some badinage and occasional mild abuse. Enlightenment, though, is in short supply. Regular attenders at Alastair Campbell's briefings acknowledge that one of his notable skills is steering newspapers towards stories of particular interest to them. Correspondents working for tabloid newspapers, where Campbell's own experience and instinct lie, appreciate these 'steers': 'He is very good, he knows what papers want. During the general election, for instance, he was very helpful to us, steering us towards stories he knew we'd like which not necessarily anyone else would want.'[23] Campbell is also admired, albeit grudgingly, by the more experienced political journalists, who recognize his skill at playing the lobby. The Political Editor of the *Sun*, for example, notes:

'Alastair [Campbell] has a very clever way at the lobby briefings of turning unwelcome questions back on the questioner, and making a joke – sometimes at the expense of the questioner, so the rest of the lobby laughs and they lose momentum. Sometimes it works, sometimes it doesn't. It's all done very lightheartedly and everybody has a lot of fun, but the person who is making the point often finds that he is swept away as everyone else jostles for the chance to ask their own questions ... journalists can never get their acts together on anything, or almost anything. It is only on a very, very big story do they try and co-ordinate their questions. So normally you'd have one person saying, "what about this" on a sort of technical question, then another one coming in before the first one had completed his point.'[24]

Briefings during the dog days of John Major's tenure at Downing Street were particularly unrewarding. This was partly because of a 'bunker' mentality which meant that Number 10 felt that the best media strategy was to say as little as possible. But journalists present at the briefings also believed that John Major's press secretaries did not have the same access to and intimacy with him as Bernard Ingham had had with Margaret Thatcher. Major's last Press Secretary, Jonathan Haslam, would respond to quizzing over the Prime Minister's reaction to the most recent scandal involving a Conservative MP, or the latest act of rebellion by anti-European Tories, with a laconically delivered 'the Prime Minister is not best pleased' or some other formulaic response. Journalists are nothing if not inventive, and, after some careful crafting, even such mundane generalities can be turned into a story. This 'crafting' can only be done by fleshing out the line from the briefing through talking to a variety of other sources: politicians, special advisers, press officers, and so on. The briefing, in other words, provides the starting point of a political story, rarely its totality.

The afternoon briefings, as part of the curious archaic traditions which surround Parliament, take place in a garret of a room under a narrow, winding corridor in a corner of the House of Commons. The fiction is that the

Prime Minister's Press Secretary has been invited into the House by the chairman of the lobby, who therefore presides. The format of the briefing is similar to that of the morning briefings except that there is very little parliamentary information to impart and far more speculation about the day's developing stories.

There are two other lobby meetings, which follow a slightly different pattern. After the normal Thursday afternoon briefing the Leader of the House, the government's business manager, comes to the lobby to give a briefing on the following week's parliamentary timetable. On Fridays, when the House is quiet and fewer daily journalists are around, a special briefing is held for Sunday newspaper correspondents which provides them with their own leads.

The news cycle

The significance of these briefings is that they represent the front line in the battle for the news agenda, a battle that is fought on an hour-by-hour basis between journalists and politicians. Political news, like most other news, is now a 24-hour process. Thus, identifying where one news cycle ends and another begins is not an easy task. However, for most journalists and politicians the day begins with the sound of BBC Radio 4's *Today* programme, with its legendary agenda-setting powers, usually accompanied by the dull thud of the morning newspapers landing on the hall floor. And for much of their working day political journalists spend their time watching and listening to politicians, watching and listening to each other and watching and listening to the electronic media. For although most print journalists are adamant that television does not set their news agendas, the sheer speed of political events means that they are beholden to television and radio, as well as the Press Association (the national news agency), to enable them to keep abreast of the changing political news environment.

For the production staff of *Today*, and other morning radio and television programmes, the 'political day' in fact begins in the latter half of the previous day when they make a series of interview 'bids' for politicians, engage in negotiations with press officers and participate in occasional rows. It is instructive to try to trace the 'average' political day as it unfolds, starting from the almost arbitrary moment of 1 a.m. The convenience of this starting time is that the news-gathering, as far as the morning newspapers is concerned, has ceased and broadcasters have moved into a new cycle (the BBC's midnight news represents a summary of the day that has just ended rather than the start of the next news cycle). By the small hours, the producers on the BBC's *Today* programme and their television equivalents at the BBC, ITV and Sky will have gained a good idea of what their upcoming programmes will contain.

Conversations will have taken place, through the previous evening, between the producers and their colleagues based at Westminster, discussing what sort of reports and packages might be filed for the next morning. *Today,* for example, frequently sets the political scene shortly after it comes on air at 6.00 a.m. with what is called the 'early two-way' – a semi-arranged conversation between the *Today* presenter and a political correspondent about the day's upcoming stories. The basis of this conversation (and questions will have been fed to the presenter in advance) is what the correspondent had learnt from his conversations the previous evening with politicians, spin doctors and others. In other words, the context within which political journalists make judgements about the significance, or otherwise, of a particular story will be one in which the views of politicians will inevitably predominate. In addition, the political correspondent's perspective, and indeed the decision as to whether or not to hold the 'two-way' in the first place, will have been much influenced by the political coverage in the morning's newspapers (these are usually available in Westminster around midnight).

The *Today* programme 'two-way' will probably be followed later in the programme by political interviews developing the theme or themes set out in the initial conversation between the correspondent and the presenter. These interviews will be monitored and responded to by other broadcasters and the evening newspaper journalists. In the course of the day the national print journalists will join the fray to add their own contribution to the mix. At the same time, the broadcasters will have had in front of them that morning's papers and will be working out how, if at all, they should be reacting to the national newspapers' political coverage.

Of course, just as broadcasters are very much influenced by the agenda of the national press, so too are those working in newspapers dependent on their broadcasting colleagues. There are certain radio and television programmes which are fixed points for political correspondents, and which attempt to rise above the clamour and find a new angle or start a new story rolling. In the category of these 'major feeder media' come, in addition to the *Today* programme, Radio 4's *The World at One*, ITN's and the BBC's lunchtime and early evening bulletins, *Channel Four News* at 7 p.m., the BBC's *Nine O'clock News* and, usually, *Newsnight* at 10.30. The minor feeder media include Sky News, BBC News 24 and ITN News (although when there is a major story breaking, most correspondents will keep a close eye on their output), BBC Radio 5 Live, *PM* and *The World Tonight* on Radio 4, breakfast television programmes and mid-week political programmes from Westminster.

The daily routine of the political reporter is arduous. In addition to monitoring the output of the broadcasters, reporters follow a daily routine that begins with scanning the competition. Trevor Kavanagh, the Political Editor of the *Sun*, sketched out the vast amount of reading he felt he needed to do every day, just to stay in touch:

'The typical day starts off very slowly and often builds to a rather nerve-racking mid-afternoon climax. It begins with reading all the papers. This is quite a long process in itself because you need to read not just your own paper but all the political stories that others have written. . . . In order to keep absolutely ahead of the game, or abreast of the game – because you never really get ahead of it – you've got to read the gossip columns, the editorials and the editorials in all the major papers. You have to read the op-ed pages [the opinion pieces and leading articles], and even the business and economics pages these days, to keep up to date with industry and relationship between industry and government. For instance, in our case we are particularly interested in the Single Currency and European Union and its financial measures, and the preparations for the Single Currency are dealt with in some interesting detail in the *FT* [*Financial Times*] and the business pages of all the major broadsheets. So you have to read all of the papers every day, listen to the *Today* programme and try and watch television at the same time. . . . and it's not just the morning papers. We also have to read the political journals, like the *New Statesman*, the *Spectator* and the *Economist*.'[25]

Reporters also have to monitor constantly the various editions of the London *Evening Standard* (a crucial platform for setting the day's news agenda); keep a close eye on the Press Association wires; attend press conferences; listen to MPs performing in the chamber or a committee; chat with MPs and others in and around Westminster; and, of course, 'do lunch'. The Political Editor of one Sunday newspaper described the importance of these occasions:

'I normally have two or three lunches a week and that is an important source of stories both in terms of what might be discussed at a lunch, [and because] it's a very important part my job to build up personal relationships of two-way trust, so with a minister, even if you don't get a story from the lunch, you feel like you are more likely to get a more positive response the next time you ring up that particular minister.'[26]

In recent years a practice has developed of 'team lunching' whereby two correspondents from the same news organization, or from organizations that are not in direct competition with each other, will take a politician out to lunch. The advantage of having two reporters present is that it not only enables them to compare notes about the significance of various statements but also prevents the politician from denying anything that might have been said but subsequently proves embarrassing. However, as Trevor Kavanagh explained, this practice has now been discouraged:

'This government doesn't like lunches with two journalists at once because they prefer the "plausible deniability" factor that comes with only a one-to-one. If there are two of you, I suppose sometimes – and I stress the rarity – [there are occasions] where the journalists have gone away and pooled notes and have perhaps pushed the story a little too far. But I think they've used that as an excuse for limiting lunches to one-to-one.'[27]

Kavanagh elaborates on how the Labour government has been seeking to exercise far greater control over the media than did its predecessor governments (see Chapter 7 for more detail):

'[T]his government doesn't like to see anything in the papers that it hasn't authorized, especially if it's a story they want to hold on to, or prefer not to see in print at all. And if anything appears in the papers or the media anywhere, there is quite a systematic attempt to track down the culprit, cross-referencing who's had lunch with whom, who knows whom, whose byline was it under, who are his known contacts, and so on.'[28]

The majority of political stories still tend to come from the various fixed points in the reporter's week. As well as twice-daily briefings given by the Prime Minister's Press Secretary, there is the weekly Prime Minister's Question Time, which, apart from providing a story or stories in itself, gives lobby correspondents a chance to pin down elusive MPs. However, political journalists' main activity is talking with MPs in the House of Commons lobbies and in the bars and tea-rooms, and conducting conversations among themselves and with the parties' media teams. At the end of all this information-gathering, and after much consultation with colleagues on their own and rival newspapers, the reporters are ready to file – usually at around 5 p.m.

Although stories could be filed from the morning onwards, reporters like to wait in case there are new developments. Nicholas Watt, the Political Correspondent of the *Guardian*, described the pattern:

'You often tend not to start writing till as late as four o'clock, which means you have to shift a lot of copy very quickly, and it's really unlike any other area of the paper, except for court reporting, where they also start producing copy later in the day. Newsdesks are always tearing their hair out saying "why can't we have your copy earlier", and you say, "well, nothing really happens here until three or four." But in fact you tend to have a fair idea of what you are doing from pretty early on in the day. . . . There are some days when it does look very quiet early on in the day and there's been many a time when I've told the newsdesk. "I'm not quite sure what I'm going to do today, terribly sorry, it's a bit quiet." Then later on in the day you find yourself writing the splash – the main piece on the front page.'[29]

The daily routines of Westminster journalists are particularly closely monitored by politicians and their press advisers because timing plays an absolutely critical role in the Westminster news production process. For example, politicians have to ask themselves whether a story should be targeted at the early edition of the London *Evening Standard* or held back for use later in the day. The politician (or his/her media adviser) has many such decisions to make. The more experienced usually get it right, but not always. One backbench MP was noted, at around 11 o'clock one evening, trying to interest political journalists in a hand-written press release he'd produced. He was on his way to the press gallery but was advised not to waste his time since none of the political correspondents would be there. Had the press release been about the resignation of the Prime Minister, then the correspondents would have scrambled for their phones and ensured that all the remaining editions of the papers, currently being printed, were scrapped and rewritten to accommodate this bombshell. The MP took the story to the Press

Association office, which eventually ran it in the small hours. It dropped onto newsdesks around the country and no one batted an eyelid. Of course, if the story is big enough, there can be an advantage in releasing news at a time that virtually guarantees a free run in the following day's newspapers. Labour MP Tony Benn, back in 1982, informed the Press Association of his decision to run for the Deputy Leadership of the Labour Party at 3 o'clock in the morning. This was still in time, just, to catch the main editions of the morning newspaper but too late to enable journalists to gather any comments or quotations critical of Mr Benn's decision.

Today Mr Benn's decision to run would not have to wait for the morning newspapers but would be broken by the 24-hour radio and television stations that now play a significant and changing role in the new political landscape.

Notes

1. Much of the material for this chapter is based on Gaber's own experiences as a political broadcaster in the period between 1978 and 1998 with BBC Radio and Television, ITN, Channel Four and Sky News.
2. John Cole (1996) *As It Seemed to Me: A Political Memoir*, p. 447. London: Phoenix.
3. E. Clapham Palmer (1952) 'The Westminster Lobby', in Phillip Gibbs (ed.) *The Journalist's London*, p. 42. London: Allan Wingate.
4. Lecture delivered to the Institute of Journalists, London, 20 February 1929. Published in *Journalism by Some Masters of the Craft* (1932), p. 73. London: Pitman.
5. A. Mackintosh (1945) *Echoes of Big Ben: A Journalist's Parliamentary Diary, 1881–1940*. London: Jarrold.
6. James Margach (1978) *The Abuse of Power: The War between Downing Street and the Media from Lloyd George to Callaghan*, p. 2. London: W. H. Allen.
7. Interview with a member of *The Times*'s political staff, March 1999.
8. David McKie (1999) *Media Coverage of Parliament*. London: The Hansard Society.
9. See Jack Straw (1993) 'Democracy on the spike', *British Journalism Review*, vol. 4, No. 4, pp. 45-54, revisited in Jack Straw (1999) 'Wanted: one bold editor', *BJR*, vol. 10, no. 1, pp. 29-34. The 'problem' of large majorities is also very much a fact of life under the Labour government following its landslide victory in May 1997. Straw's criticisms, originally framed under a Conservative government, remain equally valid under Labour. Indeed, there are many who have argued that the Labour government itself has played a major part in downgrading the importance of Parliament by announcing new initiatives and legislation through the media, rather than in the chamber.
10. Steven Barnett and Ivor Gaber (1992) 'Parliamentary committees on television', *Parliamentary Affairs*, vol. 45, no. 3, pp. 409–19.
11. Private conversation.
12. *Independent*, 10 February 1999.
13. The news that John Redwood was to challenge John Major for the leadership of the Conservative party in 1995 was first broken by the BBC's Welsh Political Correspondent, Guto Harri, who had developed good links with Redwood during his time as Secretary of State for Wales. But the closeness of this relationship can also, of course, place journalists in a situation where a choice has to be made between this long-term relationship and writing or broadcasting a story that reflects badly on a political contact. The same journalist was involved in having to decide whether to break a story nationally about a Conservative minister, Rod Richards, who had, in an interview with Guto Harri for a small-circulation Welsh-language magazine, made highly disparaging remarks about the calibre of local councillors in Wales. The correspondent decided that the story was worth breaking nationally – it caused a row, Rod Richards was embarassed and initially angry but eventually normal relations were restored.

14. Interview with a member of *The Times*'s political staff, March 1999.
15. The broadsheet newspapers have long had such correspondents and the BBC partially joined their number in 1996 when one of their political correspondents was given a particular brief to monitor the Whitehall beat.
16. Richard Crossman, one of Harold Wilson's cabinet colleagues, records in his diary Wilson's reaction to Howard's appointment: 'The Prime Minister said that this [the appointment of Howard] was outrageous and he was going to accept the challenge of the *Sunday Times*. In order to kill Tony Howard's new job he forbade any of us (and the officials as well) to speak to him.' Quoted in Margach, *op. cit.*, p. 154.
17. 'Phone bashing' is the name given to the activity of trying to track down potential interviewees for radio and television.
18. These lobby rules were first published in Jeremy Tunstall (1970) *The Westminster Lobby Correspondents*. London: Routledge.
19. Michael Cockerell, Peter Hennessy and David Walker (1984) *Sources Close to the Prime Minister: Inside the Hidden World of the News Manipulators*, p. 33. London: Macmillan.
20. Bernard Ingham (1995) 'The awkward art of reconciliation', in Peter Jones (ed.) *Party, Parliament and Personality*, p. 43. London: Routledge.
21. Interview, April 1998.
22. Interview, December 1998.
23. Interview with Henry McCrory, Political Editor of the *Daily Star*, July 1998.
24. Interview with Trevor Kavanagh, December 1998.
25. *Ibid.*
26. Interview with Andrew Grice, *Sunday Times*, January 1998.
27. Interview with Trevor Kavanagh, December 1998.
28. *Ibid.*
29. Interview with Nicholas Watt, March 1999.

CHAPTER FOUR

Broadcasters and politicians: a history of control

Television news is now the major source of information for most people, on both sides of the Atlantic. In the UK, large numbers of people watch television news on a daily basis – between 6 and 7 million each evening for the main bulletins. On days of real political significance, for example when Margaret Thatcher resigned, those audiences can rise to 12 million or more – one in three of the adult population. The Independent Television Commission has been monitoring people's news sources since the early 1970s, and its most recent data show that 62 per cent say that television is their preferred source for keeping up with national news compared with 17 per cent who say they rely on newspapers. Whatever the limitations on the number of stories and lack of detail, broadcasting's immediacy and vividness cannot be matched by the print media.

The relationship between politicians and broadcasters has usually been tense, sometimes abrasive and always subject to the most intense public scrutiny. It has never been an equal relationship, but it is becoming progressively more unequal as politicians take a firmer grip on a whole panoply of controls ranging from the highly formal such as the awarding of the BBC's charter and licence (see Chapter 6) to the highly informal myriad pressures that can be brought to bear to secure more favourable coverage, or at least to minimize damaging coverage. This form of pressure takes place within a political context that has, since the very first days of broadcasting, assumed that broadcasting has a potentially malign influence within the democratic process. It is instructive to note how politicians' complaints appear almost identical, irrespective of their politics. For example, this extract from the *Independent* newspaper:

> The Government has admitted trying to exert pressure on the BBC to toe the line in its coverage of the bombing of Iraq.[1]

comes not from 1991 when Britain, under the Conservatives, was at war with Iraq, but from December 1998 when the Labour government had joined with the United States in launching a four-day bombing strike on Iraq. The complaint echoed, almost word for word, complaints lodged by John Major's government seven years earlier; and similar complaints had been voiced a decade before that by Conservative MPs unhappy with the BBC's coverage of the Falklands conflict.

Broadcasting, bias and political control

In fact, complaints by politicians about alleged bias by the BBC can be found even before the Corporation's foundation in 1922, when the Labour-supporting *Daily Herald* complained that 'Marconi House [home of 2LO, the precursor of BBC Radio] was being used for political purposes'.[2]

It was, however, the birth of television that particularly raised politicians' anxieties. Sir Winston Churchill was dismissive of television. In discussing the so-called fourteen-day rule, which effectively restricted the BBC from covering issues of current political controversy, he said pointedly, 'I think that the liberty of the individual must be sustained against the tyrant, it must be sustained against the mass and it must be sustained against the machine.'[3]

It was his successor, Sir Anthony Eden, who took the most active role in engaging with the BBC, and for the first time ITV, about what he saw as their inherent bias. And this antagonism, which came to a head during the Suez crisis – when Britain and France invaded the Suez Canal Zone – started before any British troops had embarked for Egypt. In June 1956 Eden's private secretary wrote to Charles Hill, then the minister responsible for broadcasting, expressing the Prime Minister's concern about the BBC's alleged bias. He wrote:

> He [the Prime Minister] is a little concerned to notice that the BBC have added yet another socialist commentator [Aidan Crawley] to their staff. They seem to be leaning rather too much in that direction in recent appointments – and he wondered whether you had any views about this. I do not think that he wants anything said, or any other action taken, he simply wants to know how you feel about it.[4]

Given Hill's later crucial roles as chairman of both the BBC and the Independent Television Authority, his reply is illuminating for its odd combination of insight, naivety and understated robustness. Hill wrote:

> The BBC always leans to the left. There is something about big bureaucracies that act[s] as a magnet to the socialist planner. Add to this the Reith tradition that it is the duty of the BBC to educate and to inform, to elevate and to uplift and the lure to the left becomes even stronger. Even our own child . . . the ITA selected a socialist for its Director General [Sir Robert Fraser] . . . the left talks better, argues more fiercely and pontificates more profoundly than the right. . . . The sight and sound of a radical thumping the table thrills the public more than the sober reflections of the Conservative-minded.[5]

However, Hill's missive did not end at this point. As Postmaster General, and therefore the minister with statutory responsibility for ensuring that the impartiality clauses in the BBC's charter and licence were enforced, he offered the following suggestion to the Prime Minister:

> [D]espite what I say I am pretty sure that the BBC does not consciously and deliberately favour the left. It would probably set out to adjust the balance if there

were brought to their notice more right-minded speakers. . . . We need to deliberately seek out men, outside as well as inside the house, capable of doing this sort
of work. Let us offer them more good broadcasters from the right and hold our
direct fire until there is evidence that they reject the approach.[6]

A few days later Hill followed up this letter with something more positive.
He had just lunched with the then Chairman and Director General of the BBC
– respectively Sir Alexander Cadogan and Ian Jacobs – and had raised the
issue of the BBC's 'impartiality' and how it squared with the fact that four of
its leading commentators were all publicly associated with the Labour Party.[7]
Hill's letter continued:

At this point Cadogan and Jacob melted coyly. Yes they agreed that this looked
wrong. Their position was that they had to choose the best broadcasters, and on
pure 'merit' these happen to be left-wingers. Could we provide more candidates
from the 'right'? If so they would be glad to know of them. . . . In short we have a
clear-cut invitation to put forward new names. I learnt from Oliver Poole [chair-
man of the Conservative Party] that he is at work searching and training.[8]

The letter concluded with a note in Eden's own hand: 'Yes please and keep at
it together until you have the men and the BBC have accepted them.'[9]

Neither the BBC's archives nor the Public Record Office indicate any
record of the results of these discussions being put into effect. However, in
Eden's remaining months in office no further complaints about BBC impartiality are recorded. Shortly after Hill's lunch with Cadogan and Jacob,
Christopher Chataway, one of ITN's original newscasters, was persuaded to
jump ship and join the BBC. Chataway was, in Hill's words, 'a man of the
right.'[10] Chataway later became a Conservative MP and was himself put in
charge of broadcasting in 1970 when he was appointed Minister of Posts and
Telecommunications.

It was not just the established BBC that came under the critical scrutiny of
Eden as part of his crusade to end what he saw as the Labour Party's control
of broadcasting. The BBC, for him, was a lost cause, but the new commercial
network, ITV, and its news provider, ITN, were a different matter. However,
despite the prominent part played by leading Conservatives in the campaign
to found ITV, the first Director General of its regulatory body, the Independent Television Authority, was Sir Robert Fraser, a former Labour
parliamentary candidate. And, to add insult to Conservative injury, the
crucial post of editor of ITN also went to a former Labour MP and minister,
Aidan Crawley. Within a year Crawley had fallen out with the ITV companies and resigned. Norman Collins, an influential figure in the worlds of
both broadcasting and politics,[11] tipped off the Prime Minister about Crawley's resignation and suggested that this might be a situation that could be of
benefit to the Conservatives. Oliver Poole, Conservative Party chairman at
the time, takes up the story. In a letter to Prime Minister Eden in June 1956 (at
the same time that the PM was engaged in the hand-to-hand fighting with the
BBC described above) he wrote:

You told me at a luncheon yesterday that an appeal had been made by Independent Television News to the Conservative Party asking us to make suggestions for a replacement for Aidan Crawley but that no reply had been given. I spoke on the telephone yesterday afternoon to Norman Collins whom I know well. He told me that when Aidan Crawley had submitted his resignation from ITN that he had suggested to Sir Robert Renwood [a Chairman of one of the ITV companies] and also to Mark Chapman-Walker [Publicity Director for the Conservative Party] that the Conservative Party might informally put forward a suggestion for a suitable replacement but that no suggestion has been made.[12]

Nevertheless, the 'cock-up' rather than 'conspiracy' version of history ensured that the suggestion was never acted upon. Crawley was in fact succeeded by Geoffrey Cox, who, far from being a Conservative, was a personal friend of the then Labour leader, Hugh Gaitskell.

Eden's manoeuvrings against the BBC and ITN might be dismissed as the irrational actions of a paranoid politician, whom both contemporary journalists and historians have judged to have been a disastrous prime minister.[13] However, we now see that those early tensions set the tone for relations between politicians and broadcasters, over the succeeding forty-five years.

Broadcasting politics: Westminster

Today's political media landscape has indeed been transformed by a far greater broadcasting presence in and around Westminster. This change is physically manifested in the form of Number 4 Millbank, a mock-Edwardian building just down the road from the Houses of Parliament, housing up to 300 broadcasters. It stands as the symbol of what, for many, is the electronic media's dominance of contemporary politics – a place that MPs say they abhor and yet fall over themselves to frequent. For it is here that the radio and television studios of all the major British broadcasting networks are housed. And it is in these studios and on College Green just outside that arguably the real political dramas of the day are played out, rather than on the floor of the House of Commons. Even on those few occasions when the media's attention is focused on events inside Parliament, such as the weekly ritual of Prime Minister's Question Time, critics claim that the real power still lies with the broadcasters. As one frustrated MP said: 'Any MP can stand up in the House and say what he or she likes but it's you guys, who decide whether anything that he's said is worthy of putting on the national news, who've got the real power.'[14]

The actual televising of Parliament – the supply of the signal, as it is formally known – is undertaken by an independent production company, called CCT, which supplies continuous coverage of the Commons and the Lords to all British and foreign broadcasters. It is appointed and controlled by a joint committee of broadcasters and members of the Lords and Commons who form a majority of the supervising body and who entrust day-to-day supervision of the coverage with a parliamentary officer who ensures that the very strict rules of coverage are observed by the broadcasters. These rules include forbidding the cameras from revealing how full – or, more likely, empty – the House is, from covering any disturbance taking place in the chamber or from framing an MP in anything more exciting than the standard medium close-up shot. Committee coverage is not continuous but demand-driven. CCT establishes, a week in advance, what the various committees will be covering and then canvasses the broadcaster to find out how much interest there is in any of those hearings. Since broadcasters have to pay for this coverage on an ad hoc basis, this provides a good discipline for establishing where their priorities really lie (this is in contrast to coverage of the Commons and Lords, for which the broadcasters pay an annual fee). On an average week in 1999, CCT was covering around ten committee hearings a week.

Network television and radio programmes exclusively devoted to politics and Parliament are mainly to be found on the BBC. BBC Radio has been broadcasting *The Week in Westminster* since 1929, *Today in Parliament* since 1945 and *Yesterday in Parliament* since 1947. But the regular broadcasting of Parliament on television did not begin until 1986, when the Lords first allowed in the television cameras; the Commons eventually followed suit in 1989. When Parliament is sitting, the BBC also broadcasts a late-night daily television summary of the day's parliamentary events; a thrice-weekly afternoon programme, *Westminster Live* which consists of both live coverage of the House and interviews; and, on occasion, a daily late-night political talkshow. The BBC also transmits two weekly programmes devoted to politics, both on Sunday: an interview programme based around the personality of broadcaster David Frost, and *On the Record*, which is broadcast at Sunday lunchtime and consists of a major interview as well as feature items.

In comparison, the commercial terrestrial networks, ITV, Channel Four and Channel Five, can boast of just three networked political programmes across the entire week. Three times a week Channel Four broadcasts *Powerhouse*, a live Westminster-based political news programme. On Sundays ITV transmits two political interview programmes: one on GMTV in the early morning and a later one produced by LWT at lunchtime. The satellite channel Sky News devotes most weekday afternoons to live political coverage; it has a weekly political magazine programme on Sunday and it also shows weekly highlights of the House of Lords' deliberations. Finally, mention should be made of the Parliament Channel – a cable channel originally operated by United Artists which is exclusively devoted to transmitting live coverage of the Commons and live and recorded coverage of the Commons committees and the Lords. In 1998 it was taken over by the BBC and added to its range of digital and cable channels.

Politics plays a consistently important role on British television news, with news bulletins throughout the day on three of the five terrestrial networks and round-the-clock UK political coverage on satellite and cable stations BBC News 24 and Sky News. While Parliament is sitting, the main evening bulletins will contain on average two political stories a day on the BBC and one on ITN. In a recent study of the BBC and ITN news which sought to identify the main sources of political news on television, it was revealed that the politicians themselves were the most important single source. Reports from Parliament rarely formed stories in themselves, but clips from parliamentary debates or committee hearings would go to make up part of the political correspondent's packages.[15] A recent study by the Hansard Society of ITN and BBC bulletins has revealed that between January and March 1999 barely 4 per cent of news items involved politicians, and of this figure, less than 1 per cent contained parliamentary coverage.[16]

Broadcasting politics: party conferences

It would be mistaken to dwell on Westminster as the sole focus of political coverage.[17] Election campaigns are, of course, obvious times when the media's political gaze moves away from Westminster, but there is also a period every autumn when attention switches to the faded splendours of a series of Victorian seaside resorts and spa towns, as the political parties embark on their annual conferences. Here, relations between journalists and politicians tend to be both more intense and – away from the rigid rules of the lobby – more relaxed than at Westminster. They provide a fascinating backdrop for tracing the changing nature of the relationship between politicians and broadcasters.

For the modern political party the annual party conference represents simultaneously both an opportunity and a threat. The opportunity lies in the fact that, in theory at least, the parties have a week in which they can communicate directly with the voting public. The threat is that by putting themselves on such public view, they also have to expose to a national audience their own internal difficulties.

Party conferences take place in September and October, at the start of the political year, a few weeks before Parliament reassembles. In public relations terms these should be golden opportunities for the parties to establish their long-term priorities, announce new policies, project favoured personalities and reinforce key messages. Until the mid-1980s, conference coverage on television was significant. Both BBC and ITV (and then Channel Four) devoted many hours of daytime television to relaying the proceedings live from the conference floor.[18] The main news bulletins of the day were often presented from the conference and both the BBC and Channel Four ran nightly 'highlights' programmes summing up the day's proceedings. When a party was doing well, such PR opportunities could be well used.

In the main, the parties see the conferences as their opportunity to speak directly to the public without significant media interference, a view from which the broadcasters used not to dissent. Indeed, the late Vincent Hanna, who covered politics for BBC Television's current affairs programmes, believed that allowing the parties a chance, once a year, to address the electorate, in their own terms, was an important part of the BBC's public service broadcasting obligations.[19]

Consequently, every aspect of the conference presentation is now given detailed consideration. Many thousands of pounds are spent on consultants, designers and producers to ensure that the overall visual message of the conference reinforces the party's political message. At the Conservatives' 1982 conference, sandwiched between victory in the Falklands War and Margaret Thatcher's election victory in June 1983, the conference set featured a strangely shaped backdrop containing the slogan 'The Resolute Approach'. Close up, the set did not make a great deal of sense. However, from further back in the hall and, more crucially, in the viewfinders of the television cameras, the subliminal message struck home: the shape was that of a warship and the slogan was a subtle reference to HMS *Resolution*, which had played a key role in the Falklands War. The conference was 'produced' by Harvey Thomas, who had learnt his trade by producing rallies for the American television evangelist Billy Graham. He was in no doubt about how important it was that the visual impact of the conference was planned, with the key moment – the party leader's speech – as the central focus: 'When the Prime Minister makes that speech, we only get a few seconds on the TV news and we have got to make sure that those few seconds are absolutely pure as far as the message is concerned.'[20]

In general, relations between the media and the parties at these conferences are relatively cordial, with the parties' media offices seeing their role as, to some extent, facilitators of the broadcasting and print coverage. Television producers and conference organizers spend many months jointly planning the logistics of the conference to ensure that the watching television audience has the best sound and pictures – there being a mutuality of interest which makes such negotiations relatively straightforward.[21]

However, there has always been a significant distinction between Conservative conferences and those of Labour and the Liberal Democrats (and their predecessor parties). For the Conservatives it was always an open secret that their conference was essentially a morale-boosting rally. It was the chance for the faithful to be rewarded with a week at the seaside, to have the opportunity of rubbing shoulders with the mighty, and a moment for the party leadership to use the absence of opposition to make a string of new policy announcements. For Labour and the Liberal Democrats, annual conferences were moments of genuine democracy. Motions, which could become party policy, came up from the grassroots of the parties to be debated in front of a national audience, sometimes with embarrassing results.

But Labour learnt fast. Through the 1970s and early 1980s their annual gatherings had been occasions redolent far more of threat than of opportunity as their internal divisions were exposed to the full glare of media attention. For journalists covering Conservative Party conferences, they could be very dull affairs as a succession of ministers spelt out widely trailed announcements to an enthusiastic audience. Compared to the famine of Tory Party conferences, Labour gatherings were veritable journalistic feasts.

One of the first lessons that trainee journalists learn is that 'news is about conflict'. Confronted with a story, reporters are encouraged to ask themselves 'Where's the conflict?' The response to such a question at Labour conferences in this period might well have been 'Where isn't there conflict?' At the start of every conference session a line of constituency party and trade union activists would queue at the speaker's rostrum to take turns in denouncing either the National Executive Committee, the Labour leadership, or anyone else who might have incurred their wrath. It made for gripping television, but in terms of Labour's public relations it was a disaster. The contrast with, for example, the Labour conference in 1999 could not have been greater, perhaps symbolized by one woman delegate who returned to the speaker's rostrum one morning to apologize for embarrassing the platform the previous afternoon by calling for a vote on an issue that the leadership wanted quietly ignored.

For most political journalists the party conference begins with a press briefing on the Sunday afternoon prior to the conference's formal opening. In the period when the Labour conference was the central focus of political debate within the party, the General Secretary would go through the week's programme, outlining which proposals were likely to be accepted by the party leadership and which were to be opposed. Since at this period 90 per cent of the votes at the conference were in the gift of the major trade unions, the journalists would then troop off to the far more important series of union briefings, where the respective union leaders would indicate how their delegations intended voting on the issues coming before them.

It was all grist to the journalistic mill, but it meant that the tone of the week's proceedings was set by the sound of speculation on the airwaves (and in the press) as to which motions were likely to cause the leadership difficulties in the week to come. In terms of reporting to the electorate the genuine state of opinion within the Party, the operation could not be faulted; in terms of the party taking maximum advantage of the opportunity of a week's free advertising it was a shambles. Hence, in the late 1980s Labour began to take control of the process to ensure that it set the terms of the week's coverage. It did this in a number of ways, including forcing through changes in the party's politics, organization and presentation, but perhaps above all, in seeking to change the terms of trade in its dealings with the media.

One of the major differences between party conferences twenty years ago and today is in the effort made to control the media's agenda. Briefing of the political lobby did take place but in strategic terms little thought was given as to how the week was to be presented – what were the key themes and personalities to be projected, which lines of attack were to be pursued, and so on. The modern party conference is one long 'media opportunity'. Briefings begin weeks before the conference itself and continue, almost on a 24-hour basis, throughout the week. As well as the traditional Westminster lobby, key broadcasting producers and presenters are seen as important targets.

Some of the techniques employed by parties to influence media coverage are analysed in detail in Chapter 7, but one example will illustrate the change in party conferences. In the past, at Labour conferences, the choosing of ordinary delegates to speak at the rostrum was very much a lottery, with the chair of the conference calling on those who caught the eye. Experienced delegates who hoped to be called in debate could usually be identified in advance by the their brightly coloured clothing, which they hoped would help them get noticed by the chair. Now delegates are invited to conference training days, the ostensible purpose being to initiate them into the sometimes arcane and perplexing conference procedures. However, such gatherings also give party officials a chance to identify both potential heroes and potential villains. The former are those members of the party, frequently young and attractive and able to speak well, who can be relied on to follow the party line and stand a good chance of attracting national broadcast coverage. The latter are those delegates whose political views and opinions would be categorized as 'unreliable' (usually left-wing) and whose interventions at the conference might be predicted to be 'unhelpful'. Delegates are also trained in public speaking techniques (their training takes place both before and during conference) and are encouraged to prepare contributions to specific debates – particularly if they have some personal contribution to make (the words 'speaking as a nurse' are music to the ears of party managers). Party managers send pager messages to the chair if he or she is having difficulty in identifying 'helpful' speakers. For particularly contentious debates party workers are placed at strategic points in the hall to 'encourage' applause at appropriate moments (applause is much beloved by radio and TV producers, providing, as it does, neat editing points). Nothing is left to chance.

It is a truism the world over that politicians worry about bias against them or their party and have always taken measures to minimize or, in extreme cases, prevent it. With broadcasting, the concern is multiplied by the perceived power and popularity of the medium. What started in Britain as attempts to control who *runs* the broadcasters has gradually become a concerted – though not always successful – operation to control the political content of broadcasters. Arguably, as long as parties representing all shades of political opinion are equally successful in their techniques, democratic pluralism might still be served. Bigger problems start to emerge, however, when governments use their power and their patronage to exert political influence over ownership of the media.

Notes

1. *Independent*, 24 December 1998.
2. Quoted in Asa Briggs (1995) *The History of Broadcasting in the United Kingdom: The Birth of Broadcasting, 1896-1927*, p. 69. Oxford: Oxford University Press.
3. Sir Winston Churchill, Cabinet papers PRO PREM 11 1212, Public Record Office, London.
4. Letter from J. Bishop (Private Secretary to Anthony Eden) to Charles Hill, 15 June 1956, PRO PREM 11 1212, Public Record Office, London.

5. Letter from Charles Hill to Sir Anthony Eden, 21 June 1956, PRO PREM 11 1212, Public Record Office, London.

6. *Ibid*.

7. These were Francis Williams, Aidan Crawley, Christopher Mayhew and Woodrow Wyatt; the latter three all subsequently became Labour MPs and all subsequently left the Labour Party.

8. Hill to Eden, 29 June 1956, PRO PREM 11 1212, Public Record Office, London.

9. *Ibid*.

10. Hill to Eden, *op. cit.*, 21 June 1956.

11. In 1950 Norman Collins, who was the BBC's Controller of Television, was passed over by the Board of Governors for the post of first Director of Television. He promptly resigned and headed the campaign which five years later resulted in the launch of commercial television in 1955. During the campaign Collins developed close links with the Conservative Party and became an unofficial adviser on how the party might best exploit this new medium.

12. Correspondence, Oliver Poole to Sir Anthony Eden, 22 June 1956, PRO PREM 11 1212, Public Record Office, London.

13. For a particularly withering account of Eden's premiership, as seen by a distinguished contemporary observer, see James Margach, *The Abuse of Power: The War between Downing Street and the Media from Lloyd George to Callaghan*, pp. 100–14.

14. Private conversation.

15. Ivor Gaber (1998) 'Television and political coverage', in Christine Geraghty and David Lusted (eds) *The Television Studies Book*, pp. 270–1. London: Arnold.

16. Stephen Coleman (1999) *Electronic Media, Parliament and the People*. London: Hansard Society for Parliamentary Government.

17. The devolved assembles in Edinburgh and Cardiff are, at the time of writing, yet to have made a significant impact in terms of UK-wide media reporting.

18. In 1999 the BBC announced that the bulk of its live party conference coverage would in future be transmitted on the BBC Parliament channel, available only to cable and digital subscribers. *Guardian*, 10 October 1999.

19. Private conversation.

20. H. Thomas, from David Butler and Denis Kavanagh (1984) *The British General Election of 1983*. London: Macmillan.

21. The following account is based on Gaber's own experiences covering party political conferences during the 20 years from 1978 to 1998.

CHAPTER FIVE

Does ownership matter?

Does it matter who actually owns the media? It is arguable that from the perspective of the two conflicting social science approaches to the media – critical political economy and liberal pluralism – the identity of media owners is irrelevant. In its purest form, the first approach holds that private media will by definition uphold the basic nostrums of capitalism in which they are rooted and it matters little which particular media magnate holds the reins at any one time. And in its purest form, the second approach holds that as long as ownership is reasonably widely spread (though this is rarely quantified), private media will ensure that a proper plurality of views untainted by state interference will be available to the citizenry.

These generalized perspectives are not very helpful when it comes to looking specifically at political journalism. In terms of whether and to what extent a particular proprietor or dominant shareholder exerts influence over editorial content, there are different shades of opinion and different shades of editorial practice depending on the era and the individuals concerned. At one extreme, theoretically, is an environment where political journalism – whether news or comment – can be practised without any reference to who owns the newspaper, television or radio station concerned. Stories are judged purely on their journalistic merit according to professional criteria intern-alized by the writer or reporter concerned. They will expect their stories to be treated – and prioritized or 'spiked' – on the same professional criteria rather than according to any pre-existing political agenda laid down by a proprietor or editor.

At the other extreme, equally theoretically, is an environment where every political journalist knows that he or she is no more than a mouthpiece for the political prejudices of the owner, whether these be conveyed directly or through the offices of a compliant editor. For anything to appear in the paper or programme therefore requires that it conform to the view of the world that the owner wishes to convey. Stories will therefore be pursued primarily on the basis of whether their political line will be pleasing to the journalist's masters, and particular attention will be paid to sources known to be sympathetic to the 'correct' political line. Similarly, running stories will be written or 'spun' according to the same filtering criteria. Sanctions for not abiding by the unwritten rule of 'obey thy master' could vary from outright dismissal to an attritional process of so-called byline starvation which ensures that the journalist concerned simply never gets his or her stories in the paper. It is a moot point among professional journalists as to which is the worse fate.

In practice, both extremes are rare. The vast majority of political journalists will insist that their own operational and daily practices accord much more closely with the former model than the latter, although newspaper correspondents generally accept that they operate within a political framework set by the newspaper's ownership or tradition. Conventional wisdom among critics of the press leans more to the second model: that as ownership patterns in the press become progressively more concentrated, we are likely to see less diverse expression of opinion and more homogeneity of political reporting. These, certainly, have been the arguments behind opposition to the empire-building efforts of media entrepreneurs such as Rupert Murdoch and Conrad Black. Although usually left unstated, the implicit assumption of such opposition has been that owners have a direct influence on the political direction of their newspapers. This, in turn, makes two further assumptions about the practice of political journalism: first, that a direct and influential relationship can be traced from the political proclivities of an owner to the daily journalistic practices of a reporter. And second, that the comment and editorial pages of a newspaper – where the prejudices of an owner may be expected to appear unadulterated – cannot in practice be insulated from straightforward reporting, and that a political route-map in the former will inevitably seep through into the latter.

Even in the regulated world of broadcasting – where strict impartiality is required as a matter of law – the same assumptions apply. The massive campaign in 1999 to oppose Greg Dyke as Director General of the BBC – initiated by *The Times* and fuelled by the opposition Conservative Party – had its roots in Dyke's £50,000 private contribution to the Labour Party and an assumption that the chief executive's personal politics will find its way into the reporting fabric and political agenda of the organization. For the same reasons there was hostility towards what appeared to be the burgeoning ownership ambitions of Clive Hollick (Labour peer and owner through United News and Media of two television franchises) and Michael Green (long-standing Conservative sympathizer and chief executive of Carlton). As Green himself has said, expressing some frustration at attempts by some critics to halt a growing concentration of ownership among commercial television companies in Britain, 'Do you really think that if I went and told [the head of Carlton TV in London] what to say in his political programmes, he would take a blind bit of notice?'[1] In a move that, arguably, confirmed Green's position on the political irrelevance of ownership, these two media entrepreneurs announced in November 1999 that (subject to government regulations being relaxed) their two empires were to merge into a single media conglomerate – although the merger was frustrated on competition grounds and Hollick subsequently divested himself of all TV and newspaper interests.

On the face of it, direct and unequivocal evidence for interference in political journalism in the contemporary media is harder to find than it was one or two generations ago. It is important to put this argument in historical perspective to understand how pernicious the influence of ownership can be and how it has operated in the past. Only then will it be possible to draw sensible conclusions about how the impact of ownership may have changed and whether – and how – it operates on political journalism today.

In his book on the national press in Britain, Jeremy Tunstall argues that there has been a gradual transition from the old-style 'press lords' to what he calls 'entrepreneurial editors'.[2] Starting with Lord Northcliffe at the turn of the nineteenth century, and followed by Lord Beaverbrook, Lord Rothermere and Lord Camrose, these were men who were less interested in the money-making potential of their newspapers than in the access to direct political power which ownership bestowed: 'These old press lords did not even want to buy more newspapers; the logical way for a press lord to spend his time was in persecuting editors and politicians.' For Beaverbrook and Rothermere in particular, this persecution was not simply an autocratic approach to management, but an overt and unapologetic means of purveying their own political philosophy direct to the electorate. In particular, their views on Empire free trade during the 1920s and 1930s – completely at odds with the Conservative Party's expressed position under Stanley Baldwin – led them to challenge directly the authority of the government by supporting (both in print and financially) Empire Crusade candidates in successive by-elections.[3] There can have been little doubt in the minds not just of Conservative MPs but of those who worked for Beaverbrook's *Express* or Rothermere's *Mail* that their newspapers were instruments of propaganda and that job prospects depended on political reports toeing the proprietorial line.

In the post-war era, and particularly since the 1960s, the pattern has shifted considerably towards the entrepreneurial model. The emphasis is on acquisition and expansion across different media fields as well as across continents. For the twenty-first-century media owner, newspapers and broadcasting are part of an electronic, telecommunications or entertainment business empire and the priorities are profit maximization and keeping shareholders happy – as well as keeping potential or actual predators at bay. That is not to say that politics is irrelevant or even, in Tunstall's words, an 'amusing extra'. As we shall see, there are important areas of media policy where entrepreneurs would want to ensure that they have a minister's ear, if not a seat at the top table. There may also be burning political issues where individual owners have particular views and will exploit their access to millions of readers in order to promote their views. Finally, of course, there is the simple desirability of being close to power and being able to mix with the highest echelons of the political class. All these are important ingredients of media ownership and understandable motivations for those aspiring to 'mogulship', but they are different from the assumptions made by pre-war proprietors that they were an integral part of the ruling elite.

In addition to the cultural shift, there is the sheer weight of newsprint which new technology has made affordable to newspapers and which makes it almost impossible for any self-respecting paper to restrict itself and its burgeoning number of columnists to a homogeneous line of argument. The plurality of voices now heard in most newspapers fits better with contemporary notions of a 'marketplace of ideas' and is in stark contrast to the bygone days of political uniformity. As Colin Seymour-Ure has written,

> The sectionalisation of papers and the proliferation of columnists have slurred the familiar tones of the leader page. Papers now have editorial voices, not a single editorial voice. So a media baron's newspapers, in addition to his broadcasting properties, are gradually fitting better the plural politics of the millennium than the party politics characteristic of earlier decades.[4]

On the face of it, then, there is less scope and less inclination for proprietorial interference in political journalism in the press. The mogul continues to cast a proprietorial shadow over his media operation, but the reference points have changed and the central concern is, in the words of one chief executive quoted by Tunstall, 'marketing, maintaining your market share, promotion, and profitability'. As long as the *business* of journalism thrives and is successful, the content of journalism is less circumscribed than it was in the days of the highly politicized press lords.

This is precisely the line taken by the media entrepreneur most recently elevated to (and then demoted from) the status of mogul. Clive Hollick's entrance into the media business began only in 1990 when he launched his financial services company, MAI, into the forthcoming round of ITV franchise auctions. His bid for the south of England franchise under the name of Meridian was successful, and within a few years he added Anglia and HTV to his television portfolio as well as taking a significant stake in Channel Five. More importantly, he took advantage of the relaxation in ownership restrictions which, in 1996, allowed British media companies an opportunity for the first time to have controlling interests in both newspapers and television. Even before the relevant Broadcasting Act had been passed, MAI announced a merger with Lord Stevens' United Newspapers, which owned both the *Express* papers and the *Daily Star*. Although the resultant company, United News and Media, was supposedly a joint operation between the two previously separate companies, it soon became clear that it was to be the Hollick ascetic approach to business that was to dominate over Lord Stevens' rather more extravagant style. It was not long before the Stevens portrait which had hung rather grandly in the *Express* building on Blackfriars Bridge had disappeared from public view, and the symbolism was soon followed by the man himself.

Hollick's media empire made him the first British entrant into the business of media conglomeration. What was more unusual was his political background and affiliation. For Clive Hollick was a committed Labour Party supporter who had been an influential adviser to Neil Kinnock, the Labour Opposition leader in the 1980s and early 1990s, and had chaired the left-of-centre Institute for Public Policy Research. He was subsequently made a Labour peer by Kinnock. When Tony Blair became leader, Hollick was clearly associated with Blair's modernizing agenda for 'New Labour' and became an adviser to Margaret Beckett, the Trade and Industry secretary. Here was a great irony. After decades of complaints by Labour supporters about the 'right-wing Tory-dominated press', not only did the Labour Party have its very own media mogul, but he appeared to be a mogul in the old tradition of a hands-on, fully-paid-up member of the political class.

Hollick, however, was always clear that he was not another Beaverbrook. This may be partly because the newspapers he acquired were well established as staunch defenders of conservatism in general and the Conservative Party in particular. At the time of the 1992 General Election the *Daily Express* had been in the vanguard of some ferocious attacks on Neil Kinnock and was believed by many to have an even more slavish devotion to Central Office than its mid-market rival, the *Daily Mail*. Even those readers who were not sensitive to a newspaper's editorial direction – and they would have to be almost politically illiterate to have no inkling at all – might have been shocked into a change of newspaper loyalty if their daily paper had suddenly lurched from being a faithful follower of the right to a staunch defender of the left. That could have had serious financial repercussions, as well as marking out Hollick as a seriously interventionist proprietor. In the event, Hollick made clear in subsequent interviews that he regarded himself as a strictly hands-off newspaper owner who was happy to delegate to his managers as long as they run the operation on proper business lines. Interviewed for the *British Journalism Review*, Hollick was clear that his priority was to 'arrest a 25-year decline' in circulation, and that this involved cutting costs and investing in the paper while at the same time maintaining profitability for shareholders. He saw his role as financial rather than editorial supervision:

> The newspaper is run and operated by its management. The editor and the managing editor, both experienced, very high quality people, together with the ongoing day-to-day management, set the guidelines under which the paper is run. It will come as a disapointment to you, but I don't actually involve myself in these matters. The paper has money to invest in editorial, it has money to invest in printing, it has money to invest in promotion – all of those funds have been increased over the last year. It is up to the management of the paper to decide how they want to invest those, not me.[5]

While one might not expect an interventionist proprietor to admit publicly that he is forever badgering his editorial staff to pursue a particular line, these are hardly words that could have come from a Beaverbrook or a Northcliffe. On the other hand, there are more subtle ways in which owners will influence – if not dictate – their newspapers' political coverage. The most obvious is through the choice of editor, although Hollick again explained one change of editor on the *Daily Express* in terms of what would help the paper's circulation: 'When I decided that we wanted to make a change of gear, [I looked for] somebody who would be rather high profile, because in a modern media world the personality of the editor is an important factor.' The new editor in question, Rosie Boycott, had already established a reputation for her campaigning stance on the legalization of cannabis at the *Independent on Sunday* and – whatever her formal politics – was not renowned as a right-wing tub-thumper. It is inconceivable that any newspaper owner would put their complete editorial control in the hands of someone whose view of the world was completely at odds with their own. It is one thing to prioritize business performance and renounce any interest in editorial content; it would be quite another for a proprietor to read every day in their own mass-circulation newspaper opinions or news stories contrary to their own view of the world. Whatever the rhetoric, abdication of editorial control has its limits.

By a process of osmosis, one can also expect this influence to filter down into the hiring of senior editorial staff. One of the most controversial episodes of Boycott's early stewardship was the apparent hiring and almost immediate 'unhiring' of Paul Routledge as political editor. Routledge was distrusted by New Labour's hierarchy, being regarded as too close to certain Old Labour sympathies and, in particular, close to the Chancellor of the Exchequer, Gordon Brown. He subsequently published a sympathetic biography of Brown (with some help from 'friends of the Chancellor') and a much less sympathetic and very unofficial biography of Peter Mandelson, one of the Prime Minister's closest allies. Boycott, looking for a new political editor to give the newspaper a serious political edge, offered Routledge the job and then allegedly withdrew the offer after he had accepted. Although the precise details of what happened are obscured by accusation and counter-accusation (Boycott never denied that the offer was made and withdrawn), the incident is significant in two respects: first, that an editor of the previously arch-Conservative *Express* should have even contemplated appointing a political editor with such obvious Labour sympathies (whether 'New' or 'Old') was indicative of a new political spirit running through the newspaper; second, that an editor should so rapidly and unaccountably retract her own decision inevitably raises questions about interference. Hollick himself categorically denied any overt political guidance:

> As far as I know there are no hirings or firings of editorial staff here which in any way are prompted by, coloured by, affected by any political considerations or pressures. . . . My approach is a very simple one – you simply appoint on quality and you back quality. If Rosie decides to choose person A over person B, as long as she does so on the grounds of quality she has my full support and backing.[6]

Nevertheless, the editor does not work in a political vacuum and it is perfectly possible for an owner – particularly a politically active and committed owner – to convey the substance of representations made by senior government officials. Such conversations with editors might, to observe the proprieties, always end with 'of course, in the end it's completely your decision', but the implicit message will not have been lost. As in any employer–employee relationship, editors know that while they might be employed for their independent judgement and business acumen, they still owe their livelihoods to a politically opinionated boss. It would be astonishing if the boss's spirit – if not his writ – did not run through key staff appointments, the balance of story selection and most of, if not all, the editorial opinion. It may be a process of unobservable osmosis, but we have to conclude that proprietorial influence is not only present but pervasive.

Perhaps the best way of illustrating the importance of ownership is where both journalists and their editors can operate without any proprietorial influence at all. The *Guardian* newspaper is owned by the Scott Trust, whose only instruction to appointed editors is that they carry on 'in the same spirit as heretofore'. For political reporters, this means that the only influence on their journalism beyond their own professional values is the individual news preferences of the editor. The *Guardian* revels in its freedom to make trouble, and this is conveyed to the reporters. According to its Westminster correspondent, David Hencke,

> 'What's good is you are aware that the editor will back you and the editor actually says to me that he likes reporters who cause trouble. He thinks reporters who have never caused [any trouble] can't be very good reporters because they've not unearthed anything that's annoyed people.'[7]

It was the certainty of hierarchical support which allowed *Guardian* reporters to pursue the case of Conservative MP Neil Hamilton, whom the paper accused of lying about whether he had received benefits and cash payments in return for asking questions in the House of Commons. Under the Labour government it has been prepared to pursue other stories embarrassing to the government and Prime Minister. The support which *Guardian* reporters are confident of receiving is not always apparent on other papers, particularly when faced with a large government majority. As another of its political correspondents, Nick Watt, says:

> 'The key thing is if you know your political editor and the editor of your paper are going to stand by you and will not cave in to that sort of bullying. Then you know you are safe. Whereas there are other papers where you know you are not safe and New Labour ruthlessly exploit that.'[8]

Political reporting can and does, of course, operate independently of proprietorial influence in newspapers other than the *Guardian*. Correspondents on papers whose proprietors have a recognizable political stance are quick to point out that they do not have to operate according to some predetermined directive from above, whatever the dominant stance might be on the opinion and editorial pages. The *Telegraph* papers, in particular, have a reputation for news reporting which attempts to be both thorough and impartial, whatever the allegiances of its owner Conrad Black. According to *Sunday Telegraph* political editor David Wastell,

> 'The thing that drives the paper, the news reporting end of the paper, is simply ordinary news values above all else. . . . I know there is a sort of fashionable notion that newspapers all slavishly seek to serve some sort of political interest that the proprietors have, but it's not the way it ever feels to me.'[9]

That said, the *Telegraph* papers would be unlikely to pursue an investigation into wrongdoing by or corruption of a prominent Conservative Party member, although they have certainly been prepared to report such stories as they break. Journalists undoubtedly will look at certain stories in terms of the editor's agenda, and the *Telegraph* editor's agenda is less likely to include a determined attack on the party supported by his proprietor. In this case, it is not so much an influence that distorts political coverage as an influence that prioritizes it.

There are two more senses in which newspaper ownership can exert forms of influence on journalists at the beginning of the twenty-first century compared to the more blatant interference of the twentieth. The first concerns specific issues perceived to be of fundamental significance for the nation. The more emotionally divisive issues and ideologies which characterized certain periods in the twentieth century – notably the pre-war empire free trade debates and the 1980s battles over Thatcherite policies such as trade union reform and privatization – are much less apparent at the beginning of the new century. The shift towards more consensual and consumerist politics makes it less likely that individual owners will wish to involve themselves in personal crusades, at least on issues of fundamental political ideology (although crusades on more narrowly defined moral or consumer issues have probably become more frequent – for example, on legalization of cannabis, reduction in petrol prices or abolition of bank charges). Political support becomes a more pragmatic issue, a combination of personalities, business interests and feedback from readers.

The great exception is the one big political issue in Britain at the beginning of the new millennium which seriously divides individuals, parties and newspapers: whether the UK should join the European Single Currency. Given the fundamentally constitutional nature of this issue – wrapped up with questions of sovereignty, federalism and national identity – it is perhaps not surprising that it has already proved to be the twenty-first-century equivalent of the Irish question or abandoning the gold standard. On an issue of such elemental national importance, it is therefore perhaps inevitable that newspapers will follow an agenda which is in tune with their owners' convictions. In the case of *Express* newspapers, where before the 'merger' anyone attempting to argue the single currency case would have been thrown off Blackfriars Bridge, under the pro-European Hollick the newspapers became fervent supporters of Britain's joining. These were, of course, strictly the views of the *Express* editors, without any prompting from their owner – although, had they not been, the editors in question might have found themselves unemployed. In the case of other newspapers, like the passionately Eurosceptic *Telegraph* newspapers or Rupert Murdoch's stable, the owner's disposition virtually determines the line. For Murdoch's *Sun*, opposition to the euro is a logical extension of an editorial policy which has always been antagonistic to the European Union. It also fits naturally with Murdoch's political worldview. According to the *Sun*'s Political Editor, Trevor Kavanagh,

'I think that in the case of Rupert Murdoch he's always been in favour of small government, low taxes, entrepreneurial creativity, via the business people and the inventiveness of people individually. So in a sense you have his view. . . . I guess his American experiences and his business experiences have helped to form that.'[10]

The second form of influence is more inchoate: less a question of giving political direction and more of conveying a coherent view of the world which touches on the political but is as much moral and philosophical. Under the various Lords Rothermere, for example, the *Mail* newspapers have pursued a very explicit moral agenda centred on the sanctity of the family and objections to any policies or actions which might offend their (and by extension their readers') moral sensibilities. The labelling of the then chief executive of Channel Four, Michael Grade, as 'Britain's pornographer-in-chief' for sanctioning some risqué programmes on his channel was an example of the sometimes quite brutal manner in which editorial priorities would be shaped by the papers' value structure. This unremitting personal campaign was continued in the *Mail*'s hounding of Channel Five's then chief executive David Elstein.

Much the same is true of News International's stable of newspapers. Rupert Murdoch's influence on his newspapers is legendary, as former editors have testified (see, for example, the histories told by Andrew Neil and Harold Evans of newspaper life under Murdoch). Although Murdoch's political vision is perceived to be right-wing, his newspapers' political journalism does not follow an uncompromisingly slavish line in support of the British Conservative Party (unlike, say, the *Telegraph* newspapers). As others have pointed out, his approach is more pragmatic. Both in Australia and most recently in the UK, Murdoch has demonstrated his willingness to support Labour parties if he perceives some potential business or financial advantage in doing so. And on matters of party political support, he has repeatedly shown that he is prepared to lay down the law. As one of his longest-serving editors, Andrew Neil, has written about Murdoch's decision to switch his papers' allegiance to the Labour Party in the 1997 General Election,

> The decision to place his two Tory tabloids – the biggest-selling in Britain – behind Blair and the Labour Party was entirely Rupert's. Their editors played almost no part in the decision and many of the staff, especially on the *Sun*, were very unhappy about it. But they had no say in the matter and were never consulted.[11]

While formal party political support might vary with Murdoch's perceived corporate advantage, there are consistent messages within his newspapers that taken together constitute a coherent ideology. His most thorough – and, some have argued, hagiographic – biographer, William Shawcross, quotes Murdoch as follows: 'I would describe myself as being totally internationalist, free market, believing that most people will benefit most and the world will be a better place from having free markets. In ideas as well as goods.' Shawcross's interpretation of these comments is as interesting as Murdoch's own words: 'What this actually meant was that he thought the export of American values and products always a blessing. He loathed the strictures of feminism and the gay rights lobby.'[12]

Earlier in the book, Shawcross describes Murdoch's antagonism towards the royal family and how he was happy to sanction the kind of gossipy stories that would have been considered sacrilege in the 1960s: 'His papers constantly reflected his own republican sentiments – few opportunities to mock, criticize or shame the royal family were missed.' He also quotes Hugo Young as arguing that under Murdoch's ownership, the *Sunday Times* 'gave little space to discussions of poverty, inequality, injustice or other moral issues'. Those who have followed the Murdoch papers – not just in the UK but around the world – will recognize here the values that infuse his publications and which, when a particular issue of political significance arises, usually colour its coverage. Policies which might be interpreted as inhibiting international free trade – such as directives laid down by the European Union – are condemned, while a pervasive spirit of republicanism, anti-homosexuality and anti-liberalism in general is apparent throughout the Murdoch press regardless of editorial support for particular political parties.

More interestingly, Shawcross also offers valuable insights into the working practices through which this single proprietor conveyed his philosophy. Although he is never averse to direct interference – there are plenty of stories from editors past and present which attest to his quickness to lift the phone when necessary – he is more likely to pick senior editorial teams in his own image: governing 'by phone and by clone', according to Eric Beecher, a former editor of the Melbourne *Herald* in Australia. As well as demanding circulation increases through more emphasis on tabloid values and fewer stories on obscure faraway places, Murdoch eschewed serious investigative journalism, and particularly the kind of independent political journalism that uncovered Watergate-type political scandals. Shawcross describes an early example of the Murdoch method when in 1958 he replaced the campaigning editor of the *Adelaide News* with another who was 'much more of a nuts-and-bolts journalist':

> There were more cats up trees in Adelaide and fewer uprisings in Ankara. Murdoch had had enough of advocacy journalism. He was expanding his empire and was more interested in cash than in confrontation, in profits than in political positions. He wanted editors who were safe rather than scintillating, whom he could rely upon, however far away he might be.[13]

If any senior staff are in any doubt about their proprietor's vision of the world, the corporate summits in Aspen, Colorado, serve as periodic reminders. The standard-bearers of News Corporation are brought together from their positions around the globe and, in the words of Shawcross, 'fitted out with uniforms, debriefed and rebriefed, inspired and invigorated and sent back to their commands filled (it was hoped) with renewed loyalty to their

commander-in-chief and the sense of purpose of the worldwide organization'. It is this combination of coherent worldview and corporate
brainwashing which defines the Murdoch empire rather than the kind of
brash, brutal and often unpredictable interventions which defined much of,
say, Robert Maxwell's approach when he owned the *Mirror* newspapers. It
does not require individual scraps of evidence about particular stories being
pulled or altered to know that there is a certain uniformity inculcated in
News Corporation which applies to its political journalism as much as –
perhaps more than – any other area of reporting.

There is, then, still a great deal of proprietorial influence, even though it
might be more indirect and its motivation less party political than in previous
generations. There is one further development, also with its roots in corporate business requirements rather than political ideology, which has
potentially very serious implications for political journalism: the steadily
increasing importance of government media policy, and the importance for
proprietors of being able to influence – perhaps even dictate – that policy. For
a number of reasons, governments throughout the world have become
progressively more embroiled in making policies which impinge specifically
on the interests of media owners. Although in business and legal terms the
media industry has always been affected, if sometimes only peripherally, by
new legislation, it is only recently that the notion of a coherent body of 'media
policy' has come to the fore. As Colin Seymour-Ure has said,

> There was much policy relevant to media – fiscal, industrial relations, official
> secrecy – but it was not 'media policy'. Now, with media pouring all over the
> landscape, those old certainties have vanished. Governments know that the option
> of leaving media barons alone is no longer available. When they make media
> policy, moreover, they deal with organisations which are an instrument of their
> own accountability and cannot be handled roughly.[14]

Not only are they instruments of accountability but, as we have seen, they are
also perceived as powerful instruments of electability. Political expediency
therefore combines with a more principled caution about legislating on one
of the very cornerstones of democratic practice: a free media. Legislation on
privacy, for example, has proved impossible to implement despite some
quite outrageous intrusions into the private lives of individuals.[15] The combination of disingenuous editorial fury at a government legislating to inhibit
'the people's right to know' and the prospect of angry proprietors seeking
revenge for such a deliberate attempt to curb a very profitable niche has
stymied any progress on a privacy bill. In another area of media policy, there
was a blatant political move to curry favour with Britain's most powerful
media mogul when in 1989 Margaret Thatcher's Conservative government
allowed a loophole in its wide-ranging Broadcasting Bill, allowing Rupert
Murdoch to continue his nascent satellite television enterprise as well as
owning 35 per cent of the British national press. This was in direct contradiction to the government's own stated principles that:

Clear rules will be needed which impose limits on concentration of ownership and on excessive cross-media ownership, in order to keep the market open for new-comers and to prevent any tendency towards editorial uniformity or domination by a few groups.[16]

The White Paper's proposals for implementing this philosophy limited newspaper owners to a maximum 20 per cent stake of any television service, but deliberately excluded from this limitation any channel being transmitted from a private or non-UK satellite operation – including the Astra satellites from which Murdoch was broadcasting his Sky channels direct to the UK.[17] Murdoch's highly profitable satellite television enterprise was constructed on the back of Margaret Thatcher's political indulgence, and the Conservative Party was repaid with full-throated support from all the Murdoch papers up to the General Election of 1992.

The lesson of adapting media policy to fit with the requirements of powerful proprietors rather than political principle was not lost on a Labour Party gearing up for its assault on the Conservative Party's power base. Apart from Tony Blair's high-profile journey to Australia – at Murdoch's behest – to address News Corporation executives, there was frequent contact lower down the echelons. According to Andrew Neil,

> The extent of the ties that developed between New Labour and News Corp has never been fully revealed. In addition to regular meetings between the two top men, a network of contacts was established between senior company executives and Labour frontbenchers.[18]

Even so, the Labour Party's position on cross-ownership in the run-up to a new Broadcasting Act in 1996 took its supporters by surprise. Under pressure from media entrepreneurs, and in recognition of the increasing drive towards building media conglomerates across all communication sectors, the Conservative Party proposed a new set of rules: individuals or companies would be allowed to have a controlling interest in both television stations and newspapers as long as their newspaper ownership did not exceed 20 per cent of the national market. This disqualified Mirror Group Newspapers and – to his fury – Murdoch's News Corporation. Labour Party watchers expected it to endorse these proposals as a workable compromise, but reckoned without the determination of its leadership to demonstrate a new accommodation with influential proprietors. As the bill was about to enter its debating phase in Parliament, the shadow minister for broadcasting, Lewis Moonie, informed an informal group of Labour Party advisers that the new policy would be to advocate abolition of all cross-media controls. In the face of some astonishment at this complete reversal of the party's historical position on cross-ownership, the meeting was told that the new policy 'has come from the top'.[19]

It would be foolish to suggest that News Corporation's support for Labour at the following election followed directly from the party's change of heart on a comparatively small area of media policy. It was, however, a gesture of goodwill from a party desperate to bring 'onside' a media conglomerate which it perceived as being influential and for which it was prepared to legislate beneficially. This relatively unimportant episode was significant in two respects. First, it demonstrated that, if there had ever been any doubt, 'media policy' had now become negotiable in return for perceived political influence. Second, it showed that, again if there had ever been any doubt, proprietors could keep their reciprocal part of the deal by ensuring that political coverage of their newspapers was indeed put at the disposal of their favoured political party. The subliminal lesson for ambitious political parties was that as long as they were prepared to 'behave' – that is, to deliver a favourable operating framework for media companies – they could expect a measure of support. The reciprocal lesson for media owners was that as long as they were prepared to deliver political support in their newspapers, they could expect a measure of financial, commercial or legislative benefit. It is probably no exaggeration to say that every piece of media legislation that is now contemplated is overlain with political considerations about the possible implications for newspaper coverage.

On the face of it, these considerations are confined to ownership of the press, where there is no restriction on how partisan or opinionated publications can be. Statutory enforcement of unbiased reporting in broadcasting means that there is apparently little scope for broadcasters to curry favour with politicians or vice versa: ownership of a television or radio station would seem to confer little political leverage. While it is certainly true that broadcasters have almost no opportunity for influencing media policy to their advantage, the corollary – that politicians have little concern with policy which affects broadcasters – is certainly not. We saw in Chapter 4 some of the historical concerns articulated by politicians as broadcasting began to enter the political consciousness. In recent years, governments have shown themselves more than ready to introduce legislation which has transformed the landscape for broadcasting organizations. Indeed, the very impunity with which governments know they can manipulate the broadcasting industry, in tandem with the presumed political influence of broadcasting, has produced a welter of new proposals and calls for action which are in stark contrast to the kid-gloves treatment reserved for the press. On everything from the scheduling of ITV's main evening news bulletin to the funding formula for Channel Four and the export potential of British television, governments have wanted to have their say. Broadcasters know it, and have become increasingly aware of the power of governments to legislate against them. While they may be prevented from distorting their political reporting in a single direction, there is nothing which forces broadcasters to make life difficult or challenging for an incumbent government. In other words, the scope for self-censorship has dramatically increased.

A rare insight into how this 'chilling effect' might work was offered in 1994 by Greg Dyke, who at the time had spent the whole of his journalistic career in commercial television. (Six years later, after a spell of looking after Pearson's television interests, he was to succeed John Birt as Director General of the BBC.) Dyke's platform was the influential and high-profile McTaggart

Lecture which traditionally introduces the annual Edinburgh Television Festival in August. His theme was the changing relationship between commercial broadcasters and the state, and in particular the way that broadcasters were increasingly becoming supplicants: 'I fear the relationship between broadcasters and government is becoming a dependent one, with broadcasters constantly wanting favour and legislative action from Government'.[20] His concern was not the direct threats of intervention or retribution which had sometimes been provoked (particularly during the 1980s under Margaret Thatcher) by a critical or sensitive piece of investigative reporting. His concern, rather, was directed at 'the business ambitions of some of the ITV companies' which meant they were always seeking or preparing to seek some regulatory favour from government which threatened a politically free broadcasting system because of the power thereby invested in the government of the day. He gave an interesting example from the inside. The previous year ITV companies – led by the two biggest operators, Granada and Carlton – agreed that they would propose changing the time of their flagship news bulletin *News at Ten* to free up more time for entertainment programming. At the same time, however, Carlton and Granada were lobbying the government to change the ownership rules so that they could be allowed to expand their share of the commercial television empire. Politicians do not like news bulletins being moved out of peak time, especially bulletins in which they frequently feature. According to Dyke, when it came to arguing the case for moving *News at Ten*, the top men at Granada and Carlton 'disappeared without trace from the public debate'. He continued with a very revealing snippet of information:

> [T]he then Secretary of State for National Heritage, who no doubt was under pressure on the issue from the Prime Minister, added a hand-written note on a letter to [chairman of Carlton] Michael Green about changing the ownership rules which said effectively that he wasn't helping his ownership aspirations with plans to move *News at Ten*. It worked. *News at Ten* stayed at ten, the ownership rules were changed, and Carlton was able to buy Central and Granada able to buy LWT.[21]

In this case the government's will might be interpreted as benign. But what if the quid pro quo had been not the maintenance of an existing news bulletin but the exclusion of a critical documentary? Dyke commented at the time on the number and frequency of issues on which commercial television might wish to lobby government, and political and technological change has meant that the process has accelerated since then. Whether it be the size of the ITV levy to the government, the regulatory requirements still laid down by the Independent Television Commission, resisting privatization for Channel Four or trying to prevent a digital 'levy' on the licence fee which might inhibit take-up of commercial digital television, there are a seemingly never-ending number of issues on which governments can legislate, or at least threaten to legislate. Barely has one Broadcasting Act received the royal assent than speculation begins about the content, timing and potential beneficiaries of the next one. And with that kind of threat permanently hanging over commercial broadcasters, in Dyke's words 'it will take a very brave ITV broadcaster to make or broadcast a controversial programme about government if by doing so it believes it is seriously threatening its chance of persuading the Government to change a particular piece of legislation'. What is true for ITV is equally true for Channels Four and Five and even more so for the new breed of digital channels with limited resources and limited life expectancy in a highly competitive marketplace.

The classic and oft-quoted example in Britain of a commercial broadcaster being prepared to take on the government was the broadcasting by Thames Television in 1988 of *Death on the Rock*, which challenged the government's account of how three IRA terrorists were killed by the SAS in Gibraltar. After some painstaking investigative journalism, it came to the implicit conclusion that security forces might have been pursuing a shoot-to-kill policy more reminiscent of an authoritarian police state than a civilized democracy. The programme so infuriated the government that the Foreign Secretary personally tried to persuade the regulatory body, the Independent Broadcasting Authority, to prevent the programme from being transmitted. The IBA stood firm, the programme went out, and the Prime Minister was livid. At the time, the options for revenge were limited, although it has occasionally been suggested (wrongly) that the radical overhaul of commercial TV licence allocation and the failure of Thames to have its licence renewed under the new system were a direct result of that programme. More important was the demonstration by a privately owned television station that it was prepared to pursue an independent investigation in the full knowledge that it would provoke the undisguised wrath of a powerful government. It could instead have kept quiet and spent its money on making a high-rating quiz show while maintaining harmonious relations with the ruling party. But, as Lord Windlesham said after writing his independent report on the programme,

> If the price of harmony is to leave sensitive subjects alone; to ask no awkward questions; to take no risks incurring official displeasure on issues of high public importance; then it is a price set too high. Far from being a symptom that something is wrong in the body politic, I regard periodic rows between governments of whatever colour and broadcasters as genuine marks ... of a free society.[22]

An interesting case study of the way in which governments can seek revenge on media owners for challenging their authority by targeting their broadcasting interests comes from the country with perhaps the strongest and most constitutionally enshrined tradition for free speech: the United States. In her description of the unfolding Watergate revelations by the two *Washington Post* journalists ultimately responsible for toppling the President, the *Post*'s owner, Katharine Graham, offers some fascinating insights into how even the freest of free markets can be vulnerable to government intimidation. She describes how, as the *Post* started to break the story during the last few months of 1972 just as Richard Nixon was seeking re-election, the White House pressure on the *Post* to stop reporting Watergate became 'intense and uncomfortable'. She was indirectly warned by Henry Kissinger that Nixon wanted 'to get even with a lot of people' once he was re-elected.[23] The White House had been checking just before the November presidential election when the television licences owned by the *Post* were due for renewal. Graham continues, 'Of all the threats to the company during Watergate – the attempts to undermine our credibility, the petty slights, and the favoring of the competition – the most effective were the challenges to the licenses of our two Florida television stations.' Both stations had perfectly good reputations for integrity and quality, but the risk was significant and the financial impact immediate: the company saw its value cut in half in the weeks following the challenges, from $38 dollars a share to $16. Add to that the legal costs of defending the licences and the effect on morale as staff contemplated the prospect of closure, and the sum total was a very effective politically inspired assault on Graham's media assets. What emerges from Graham's first-hand account is the potentially fatal threat to the company she controlled and the vital importance of her steadfastness in the face of those threats. Reflecting on her role, she says (in a rather understated manner): 'What I did primarily was stand behind the editors and reporters, in whom I believed. .... My larger responsibility was to the company as a whole – beyond the paper – and to our shareholders.' There is a contradiction here since she is quite clear that – whatever her commitment to the truth – luck was important in unravelling the Watergate conspiracy and that 'luck was on our side'. Given the potential ruin to both the paper and the Washington Post Company, this is an extraordinary admission from its proprietor and raises the fundamental question about the influence of media ownership throughout the world: how many owners would be prepared to risk the survival of their empire on a quest for the truth, however momentous the crimes they are attempting to expose?

It is a particularly apposite question to ask of British commercial television, which throughout the 1970s and 1980s could claim a number of important investigative triumphs in the political and judicial field, to the great displeasure of governments of the time. With a plentiful stream of revenue from its advertising monopoly, and protected by a regulator which acted (as in *Death on the Rock*) as a buffer between a bullying government and inquiring broadcaster, there were no commercial disincentives to digging up inconvenient political truths. In the new era of intense competition for advertising revenue, the constant seeking of political favours and the absence of any buffer, it is much less likely that a commercial company would have any appetite for making waves. What remains is an almost unconscious self-censorship in covering difficult political stories which, inevitably, will spread even to the technically protected Channel Four as it seeks to head off the persistent threats of privatization. It is unlikely that a British prime minister would be as single-mindedly bent on exacting revenge from a media company as Richard Nixon, but there are sufficient levers of power and influence for such overt displays of muscle to be unnecessary. The 'chilling' effect is now integral to a highly commercialized and profit-oriented system.

What is true indirectly of commercial television is true directly of the BBC. There is no question that, compared to its equivalents around the world, the BBC has an enviable record as an independent publicly funded broadcaster where political reporting can – most of the time – operate impartially and offer unbiased analysis of government and opposition positions, and undertake investigations which can embarrass incumbent governments. There is equally no question that there are sufficient mechanisms of influence and control which connect the BBC directly to government and which have ensured over the years that the BBC approach to political reporting has never been entirely free from the shadow of government influence. This has been particularly true since the 1980s, when a combination of straitened economic circumstances and an ideological government with deep-rooted objections to the public sector placed the BBC's very survival in jeopardy. While governments over the years have (as we have already seen) always sought to influence the BBC, the three main levers of control were exploited more ruthlessly in the 1980s than ever before.

The first lever, inevitably, was the licence fee. Although always at the discretion of the government, the BBC had benefited throughout the 1970s and early 1980s from the transition to colour television and the more expensive colour licences. That additional stream of revenue started to peter out in the mid-1980s just as the Conservative government reached the peak of its powers and the height of its impatience with a public body funded through a regressive tax. Once the Peacock Committee had failed to recommend commercial funding as a 'solution' to the BBC, the government turned its attention to fixing the licence fee at no more than the rate of inflation and thereby prevented any further growth in revenue. It was within the government's powers, at any time, to set the licence fee at below inflation or freeze it altogether.

The second lever was appointment of the chairman and board of governors. Throughout the Conservative Party hegemony of the 1980s there was little pretence at bipartisan selection, and a long-standing tradition that the chairman and vice-chairman should be from two competing political parties was breached when the arch-Thatcherite William Rees-Mogg took over the vice-chairmanship in 1981. Candidates who did not have sympathetic party credentials were routinely rejected, giving the body responsible for the strategic direction of the BBC a distinct right-wing bias.[24]

The third lever was a review of the constitutional documents under which the BBC operated and which defined its purpose: the charter and licence. These were periodically renewed, usually every ten or fifteen years, and the charter awarded in 1981 was due to run out at the end of 1996. The internal process of reviewing and working towards renewal of the BBC charter was initiated by the then Director-General in February 1991, and almost every strategic and programming decision taken by the BBC thereafter tended to be viewed in the light of charter renewal. There had never previously been much doubt about the BBC's survival, whatever antagonism the BBC had faced from governments in the past. But against a backdrop of more intense competition, the arrival of satellite-delivered multi-channel television, a hostile political philosophy and a Conservative-dominated press which took great delight in hounding the BBC, survival was no longer taken for granted. Only once the government White Paper on the future of the BBC was published in 1994, and the conditions for a new charter laid out the following year, was survival assured. By that time, a Director General had been summarily sacked after a series of politically inspired attacks and complaints by the Conservative government.[25] It was almost certainly the longest period of sustained political hostility the BBC had ever faced.

It would have been impossible under such pressurized circumstances for the BBC's political journalism to have remained untainted by government influence. The process was never anything as crude as overt censorship, but every programme-maker and journalist was aware that senior government figures were scrutinizing BBC output for the slightest sign of what they might interpret as 'bias' and that complaints would be swift, robust and directed at senior management. One producer on the BBC's flagship current affairs programme *Panorama* said of the programme:

> There was an enormous sensitivity about what *Panorama* was up to: are we going to offend the government, are we going to cause a great deal of fuss? So that meant if you had a sensitive programme . . . you had people crawling all over it.[26]

The result, again, was a 'chilling' effect on journalistic inquiry and what Michael Grade, who became chief executive of Channel Four after moving from the BBC, famously called the BBC's 'pre-emptive cringe'. Journalists thought very carefully before advancing ideas that would involve confrontation with the government, and senior executives thought very carefully about sanctioning them.

Occasionally there was more dramatic evidence that a code of self-censorship was being imposed from above. In January 1991 a well-researched and factually correct *Panorama* was due to be transmitted, detailing how British machine-tool manufacturers had been illegally exporting to Iraq equipment destined to be made into a massive 'supergun' which could inflict major damage on neighbouring countries. The programme was due to go out just as the ground war in Iraq was about to start and was blocked by the Deputy Director General, John Birt. The details were too sensational to keep secret, and were soon leaked to a tabloid newspaper. They then appeared in a less-substantial programme on commercial television. A year later, just as the 1992 general election campaign was about to take off, the BBC's respected economics editor, Peter Jay, put together what was generally regarded as a thoughtful and impressive programme analysing the root causes of the recession in which Britain then found itself. Once again, this was felt by the BBC hierarchy to be too sensitive and once again transmission was prevented.[27] It would be wrong to treat such examples as indicative of a craven and cowed BBC, so intimidated by its recent experience that it is now unwilling to embark on any critical examinations of incumbent governments. Equally, it would be wrong to hold up the BBC as a shining example of unfettered autonomy, able to challenge governments without fear of the consequences. In one sense, starting with its coverage of the General Strike, the BBC's position has always been one of compromised independence. The question for our analysis is whether those compromises have become more frequent and are more institutionally ingrained than previously.

For structural rather than institutional reasons, the answer almost certainly is yes. It is not that the levers of influence outlined above have changed, nor that the particularly harrowing experiences of the 1980s have necessarily left a legacy of more timid, less enterprising journalists. What has changed is the competitive environment in which the BBC operates and the growing pressure on public broadcasters around the world to justify their existence and their funding in the midst of channel proliferation and technological change. Arguments about quality, diversity and innovation – which are the bedrock of the public service case – are sophisticated and becoming more difficult to put across in a political environment where governments throughout the world are seeking to cut back on public spending or (in the case of the licence fee) on the tax 'burden' placed on individuals. When a more complex political argument is allied to the growing willingness of competitors to see the BBC discomfited and to politicians convinced of broadcasting's influence over voters, it is almost inevitable that completely unencumbered political journalism within a publicly funded body becomes more difficult. The Labour government elected in 1997 has in many respects been more sympathetic to the need for and existence of a healthy BBC than any government since the 1970s. There is certainly not the visceral antagonism to the institution or its funding that characterized most of the 1980s and early 1990s: the Secretary of State for Culture, Media and Sport, Chris Smith, who has had responsibility for broadcasting since the 1997 election, has made clear his own and his government's support for the BBC.

None of this, however, has prevented the government's ministers and media advisers from sustained attempts at intimidation in the face of coverage they regard as unfavourable. In a telling incident in his chronicle of the 1997 election campaign, BBC reporter Nick Jones tells of how the shadow Chancellor's adviser, Charlie Whelan, ensured that two words he objected to in an early news report were dropped in subsequent bulletins. Jones records Whelan's undisguised joy when they met later in the day and Whelan's verdict that 'That shows bullying the BBC does work.' According to Jones, a colleague of Whelan's standing nearby echoed those sentiments: 'Of course bullying the BBC works. That's why we do it. We know it works. Obviously, in the end, the newsrooms give in, that's why we keep it up.'[27] Even allowing for the traditional braggadocio of government insiders, Jones' accounts are sufficient evidence of a Labour government prepared to use its majority and its muscle to berate the BBC into providing more favourable – or, in its own terms, more 'neutral' – coverage. Given that the BBC's funding, structure and very existence are a matter of political will, and given the very different media environment in which it will be operating, it is unlikely that the prospects for political journalism at the BBC are going to improve.

Thus, in the public and private sector, in print and in broadcasting, ownership and institutional pressures on political journalism appear to be moving in the same direction. While newspaper owners appear to have moved beyond the glaring partisanship of the days when newspapers were an integral part of the political establishment, owners still exercise a major influence over political content. They often protest otherwise, and certainly the corporate demands of a profitable enterprise are now a vital aspect of how a newspaper is run. Nevertheless, however indirect the approach and however many columnists of differing political hue are employed, the owner still makes his mark. Meanwhile in broadcasting, the scope for genuinely challenging political journalism which involves time, commitment and resources is diminishing rapidly. Even in the realm of everyday reporting, the BBC is probably more browbeaten than ever before, and the commercial sector is certainly more reliant than ever before on governments which can assist or hinder its expansion plans and commercial viability. It is not that owners or institutions are directly preventing their reporters from finding or publishing the 'truth'. It is simply becoming less worthwhile to take commercial risks or, in the BBC's case, institutional risks to achieve that truth.

Notes

1. Conversation with Barnett, June 1996.
2. Jeremy Tunstall (1996) *Newspaper Power*, pp. 79ff. Oxford: Clarendon Press.
3. Ralph Negrine (1994) *Politics and the Mass Media in Britain*, 2nd edition, p. 48. London: Routledge.
4. Colin Seymour-Ure (1998) 'Harlots revisited: media barons and the new politics', p. 11. Reuters Foundation Iain Walker Memorial Lecture, Green College, Oxford.
5. Bill Hagerty (1999) 'Citizen Clive', *British Journalism Review*, vol. 10, no. 1, pp. 19–28.
6. *Ibid.*
7. Interview, June 1998.
8. Interview, March 1999.
9. Interview, April 1998.
10. Interview, December 1998.
11. Andrew Neil (1996) *Full Disclosure*, p. xxiv. London: Pan Books.
12. William Shawcross (1992) *Murdoch*, p. 550. London: Chatto & Windus.
13. *Ibid.*, p. 102.
14. Seymour-Ure, *op. cit.*, p. 8.
15. Geoffrey Robertson (1993) *Freedom, the Individual and the Law*, 7th edition. London. Penguin.
16. *Broadcasting in the '90s: Competition, Choice and Quality*. The government's plans for broadcasting legislation. HMSO, November 1988.
17. This was justified by Broadcasting minister Timothy Renton on the spurious grounds that 'No Government can stop British newpaper proprietors buying into overseas transmitters that have been linked to non-DBS services that are not controlled by this country' (speech to House of Commons, 19 May 1989). In the same Act, the British government ensured that there were measures to 'proscribe' channels offending against taste and decency.
18. Neil, *op. cit.*, p. xxii.
19. Notes taken by Barnett, who was present at the meeting.

CHAPTER SIX

The consequences of competition

Writing about a conference entitled The Media and Public Confidence held early in 1999, the *Guardian*'s media commentator, Roy Greenslade, found widespread concern about the impact of unfettered market capitalism on the media. Given how fervently the free market was now being embraced by all parties, he wrote, with some irony, 'what a surprise it was to attend a conference last week in which journalists and politicians who have long preached the market's virtues voiced their concerns about its vices'.[1] He continued, '[A]nxiety about market freedom permeated a series of debates about ethical standards. . . . [I]t proved to be an unusually absorbing opportunity to watch numerous supporters of modern capitalism recoil at the culture it had spawned.' From Greenslade's report of this conference, it appears that this critique of capitalism extended to a generalized condemnation of falling cultural standards, but that '[n]owhere, asserted most speakers, was this clearer than in the output of the media, both in print and broadcasting'.

Allegations of 'dumbing down' in the media have been a familiar refrain of the late 1990s, but this was the first explicit acknowledgement that senior media professionals were themselves attributing a major part of the blame to an increasingly ferocious competitive environment. Some media academics from the old school might be forgiven a few wry smiles for this seemingly Damascan conversion to a perspective that has been vigorously argued in a few Marxist outposts of academe for at least thirty years. It does, however, raise the question about what has changed. After all, competition has been an integral and generally healthy component of the media landscape since the foreign correspondents of the fictional *Daily Beast* and the *Daily Brute* battled to be the first to bring British readers the latest from the African Republic of Ishmaelia. Journalism, whether it be foreign reporting, sports reporting or political reporting, has thrived on a competitive atmosphere which – according to conventional wisdom – has acted as a catalyst for genuine scoops, brilliant writing and new insights. And vigorous competition has also, historically, had a negative impact on quality which is not confined to the recent past. As Matthew Engel has written in his history of the popular press:

> [J]ournalists under pressure to get stories into the newspaper and make a living have always distorted the truth . . . : sometimes knowingly, sometimes wilfully, sometimes through incompetence – sometimes just through the editorial process

by which a complex and maybe contradictory sequence of events has to be transformed at high speed into a simple, readable, enticing headline. Freelance journalists want to get paid; staff journalists want to stay paid. It is so today; and it was no different in the 1950s.[2]

Later in his book, Engel specifically identifies the 1930s and 1980s as particular eras when papers were scrapping for every last sale, compared to the 'pre-Murdoch 1950s and 1960s or the United States in the 1990s'. On the face of it, the end of the twentieth century has simply been an extension of that super-competitive 1980s era.

And yet something is different, if the collective self-doubt of some of the nation's senior editors is to be believed. So the question which this chapter sets out to answer is: how, precisely, has competition changed in both press and broadcasting, and what has been the impact specifically on the fairly narrow field of political journalism? There are at least five interrelated changes which, taken together, define a different kind of competitive environment.

The new competitive environment

The first is a declining marketplace in newspapers. Although the scale of the decline does not even approach the apocalyptic free fall that some commentators have suggested, there was certainly a steady decrease in national newspaper sales over the twentieth century. It has been more marked among the tabloid 'red-tops' than the mid-market or broadsheet newspapers, but throughout the industry there has been a long-standing perception that editors have to fight harder and watch their backs with greater vigilance than ever before. The sense of a declining readership is exacerbated by the recognition that other, faster sources of broadcast and electronic news are metamorphosing the role of the newspaper from being a medium of news to a medium of entertainment, analysis and commentary.

Pessimists in the newspaper industry believe that further inexorable decline is inevitable as the electronic generation gradually replaces the hard-copy generation, conjuring up images of commuters plugging their newly purchased news software into their flat-top news-puters on the daily ride into work. Optimists (and opticians) are inclined to believe that the printed page is easier on the eye and a more flexible medium. Perhaps more threatening to the newspaper industry, ironically, is the sheer scale of today's newspapers compared to ten or twenty years ago. In an era when time appears to be at a premium, the twelve-section 100-plus-page Sunday paper – or its Saturday stablemate, which on a slow weekend might be three sections shorter – is unlikely to encourage the purchase or reading of more newspapers.

Simultaneously, the number of broadcasting and electronic outlets is increasing exponentially. It is easy to exaggerate the impact of new technologies such as multi-channel television and the Internet because, while information supply may be plentiful, the number tuning in to such channels or making regular use of the Internet is still relatively small. Nevertheless, in terms of its impact on political journalism, it is the supply of new sources of news which is most significant. Not only are there now three dedicated news channels in the UK, but the number of Sunday lunchtime political programmes on terrestrial channels as well as Internet news sites and more radio stations makes for a surfeit of opportunity. Almost certainly there is more space given to politics (in some form) over the airwaves or through the computer cable than has ever been the case before.

The second change is a progressively more relaxed regulatory environment in broadcasting. While the newspaper industry has always been a bastion of free-market liberalism, staunchly (and successfully) resisting any attempt to impose statutory obligations, broadcasting has traditionally been highly regulated. Until 1992 the old Independent Broadcasting Authority laid down criteria for the volume of peak-time current affairs on commercial television, and made it clear that it expected a range of political material to be covered. The ITV companies responded positively, partly because they were historically imbued with a public service ethos about the journalistic responsibilities of television, and partly because their licences to broadcast depended on convincing the regulator that they were providing a high-quality, diverse service. Meanwhile, Channel Four was protected by a statutory duty to be diverse, with its funding based on a compulsory levy from ITV. There was therefore no competition for commercial revenue.

Under the terms of the 1990 Broadcasting Act, itself a legacy of the Thatcherite 1980s, the emphasis shifted suddenly in 1993 to the creation of a competitive marketplace in commercial television. A 'lighter touch' Independent Television Commission with fewer powers of patronage replaced the IBA, Channel Four became an independent company competing for commercial revenue with ITV, and ITV companies were themselves forced to bid large sums of money in a competitive auction for their licences. Although they are not suffering financially, the harsher competitive climate in which ITV companies now operate inevitably means greater emphasis on ratings at the expense of range. This shift is exacerbated by the shift in regulatory culture. Unlike the IBA, the ITC has no role in fostering quality but simply monitors retrospectively. There are no brownie points for offering anything more serious than the barest minimum of two news bulletins and an hour of current affairs at any time. Even the scheduling decisions that were still within its power – like the mandatory half-hour bulletin at 10 p.m. which every ITV company signed up to in its licence application – have been eroded by the commercial arguments advanced by ITV companies.

When the ITC finally conceded that *News at Ten* could be moved on an experimental basis to 6.30 p.m. in order to free up valuable peak time, it was widely seen as surrendering to inevitable commercial pressure.The principle which was enshrined in a statutory slot for ITV news – that audiences should have access to news at different times of the evening regardless of the commercial interests of television companies – was seen as increasingly anachronistic in an age of multi-channel television. Although a predictable consequence of deregulatory pressures, it was nevertheless a depressing outcome for the political reporters of ITN, who had benefited from the higher profile which a late evening slot gave them. The ITC's subsequent decision to insist that ITV bring back a 10 o'clock bulletin – because of a 14 per cent drop in news audiences – was seen by many as a temporary reprieve.

While the first two changes are indisputable, the third change is less certain. It has become a conventional wisdom that there is widespread and increasing disillusionment with politics, particularly among the young. Usually cited in evidence are the dismal turnouts in local and European elections (although turnout has to date remained above 70 per cent for national elections), shrinking memberships of formal political parties, and occasional polls in which different occupational groups are 'graded' for such virtues as trust, honesty and usefulness to society. While doctors and the clergy generally score well, the public's contempt for politicians is measured by their position in the league table below estate agents – and almost as low as journalists. The most authoritative measure of public opinion, *British Social Attitudes*, concluded recently that 'Britain still appears to have low levels of confidence in both its political system and its politicians'.[3]

Despite apparently declining levels of participation, trust and interest in traditional (and orthodox) forms of politics, there is evidence that interest in more unconventional political forms is on the increase. In other words, participatory forms are changing rather than declining for a number of structural and demographic reasons. Mark Evans has highlighted a number of areas in which there has been heightened interest and campaigning in Britain recently, the most obvious being environmental protection issues. He quotes some spectacular membership increases in organizations such as Greenpeace (up from 50,000 in 1985 to 411,000 in 1993), Friends of the Earth (27,700 to 230,000 in the same period) and the Royal Society for the Protection of Birds (390,000 to 850,000).[4] In addition, the 1990s witnessed a surge of environmental protests around individual road-building schemes, often involving some strange alliances between twenty-something anarchists and sixty-something Tory women determined to prevent large tracts of country-side being turned into motorways. Other campaigning issues which have embraced a growing number of activists include human rights, animal rights, homelessness, various medical charities and campaigns arising out of national or international tragedies. The 'Snowdrop' campaign to ban hand-guns in the UK, which arose out of the killing of sixteen schoolchildren in Dunblane in 1996, succeeded in persuading the new Labour government to make handguns illegal in Britain.

It is therefore a dangerous and unproven assumption to suggest that interest in political matters is in terminal decline, and presupposes a narrow, orthodox definition of politics as the concern of formal political parties. This is important when it comes to assessing media organizations' *perceptions* of political interest in a competitive environment. Editors and media owners, for many of whom consumer satisfaction takes priority over any notion of performing an important democratic role, may be making decisions about viewers' and readers' interest in political issues based on a rather outdated interpretation of what constitutes things political. Those perceptions are, of course, greatly reinforced by the huge communications machinery now associated with political parties, which are always quick to draw attention to any watering down of coverage of their own activities. Their displeasure would not be dissipated by claims that citizens are more stimulated by single campaign issues than by the humdrum daily (and carefully orchestrated) activities of political parties. While in theory all media will pursue their own definition of the audience interest impervious to challenges from elected politicians, in practice the daily contact between journalists and politicians must influence journalistic experience of the political realm. The effect is to reinforce a conventional definition of politics, despite evidence that in this respect there *is* growing lack of interest.

The fourth change is the corollary of a system in which increasing numbers of media outlets compete for fragmenting audiences: a proportionate increase in the power of advertisers, whose money supports most of the non-public service channels. This is not an area which has received much attention in Britain, partly because the broadcasting system was insulated from competition for advertising until 1993. In the United States, the influence of advertisers in a highly competitive system has been better documented, in particular by those who have sought to demonstrate the essentially conservative and consensual values which such pressure exerts. Thus, the 'propaganda model' of Herman and Chomsky portrays advertisers as wanting 'to avoid programs with serious complexities and disturbing controversies that interfere with the "buying mood" '.[5] In addition, they and other commentators emphasize the growing importance of audience 'quality' – in other words, the importance of appealing to viewers with high disposable income. This has been echoed in Britain by the three commercial terrestrial channels – ITV, Channel Four and Channel Five – whose strategy since the onset of serious competition has been to attract the seemingly elusive category of 'AB males'. Although this is not new, the connection between a certain kind of audience, a programme environment congruent with advertising, and the content of news programmes has never been explicitly made.

It is possible that British journalistic culture is more impervious to this sort of pressure than American. It is more likely that such impacts have not yet had time to surface, or are emerging in more subtle forms. We have not yet heard of the British equivalent of the Air Canada notification to newspaper advertising managers in 1978 that its ads would be cancelled 'as long as any news story of an Air Canada crash or hijacking ran in the paper and if its ads were carried within two pages of a news story of any crash or hijacking on any airline'.[6] In terms of straight political reporting, the scope for this kind of advertiser influence is small: the proceedings of Parliament, or the announcement of government policy initiatives are unlikely to interfere seriously with a 'buying mood'. On a wider interpretation of political news, however – to include, for example, allegations of serious environmental damage against

large petroleum companies or of negligence against major chemical manufacturers – it is more plausible that in future serious stories might be changed,
demoted or dropped in deference to the growing might of advertisers in a
competitive climate.

The impact of competition

Taken together, the declining market in newspapers, massive expansion in
electronic outlets, deregulation of broadcasting, perceived decline in the
attraction of political issues and the rise in the power of advertisers have in a
number of ways transformed the nature of political journalism. First, there is
the impact on budgets. A declining newspaper market – particularly in the
tabloid sector, where cover-price revenue more directly determines income –
means editors and proprietors being forced to cut costs. Writing about the
shift in reporting standards, former editor of the *Independent on Sunday* Ian
Jack calculated that 'a reasonably productive staff reporter on a Sunday
newspaper' might write 90,000 words a year, many of which will end up on
the spike. On top of a not over-generous reporter's annual salary of £40,000,
there would be expenses, overheads and employment costs: 'Perhaps a total
annual cost to the company of £60,000 for perhaps 80,000 published words.
More than a dollar a word! You might get Gore Vidal at that rate.'[7]

Such simple calculations demonstrate how cost-cutting leads inevitably to
the rise of the uncommitted freelance at the expense of the staff reporter.
While the benefit shows up in the balance books, the losses are invisible. It is
simply not possible for a freelance working on ad hoc projects and paid by
the word to invest the same dedication, painstaking and sometimes laborious
research, fostering of valuable contacts or accumulation of expert knowledge
as a staff reporter. Many insiders in the newspaper business have remarked
on the rise of the confessional column (unflatteringly known as 'me journalism'), where readers are treated to the many tribulations of life as a
parent/grandparent/supermarket shopper/hospital patient/victim of road
rage, etc. Where such columns simply complement rather than dilute other
branches of journalism, nothing is lost. The fear is that the expansion in
column inches has – for cost reasons – been mirrored by a contraction in the
number of permanent reporters who have the time, commitment and
employment security to ferret out information rather than sub-edit press
releases.

This irony of opportunities for reporting politics being inversely propor-
tional to the quality and quantity of its provision is exactly mirrored in
broadcasting. More channels, programmes and outlets should offer more
scope for political inquiry rather than less. Once again, however, this vast
array of new opportunities also means increased pressure on the broadcasters' cost base. Here we can see the impact of the deregulatory philosophy
of the Thatcher years, with ITV, Channel Four and Channel Five all competing for a barely increased pot of advertising money. It is easy to forget how
recently and how suddenly broadcasting has changed from being a relatively

protected public sphere to a market-led model. Channel Four did not gain commercial independence until 1993 and Channel Five was launched in 1997. Consequently, the full force of a headlong dash for ratings and cost-cutting pressure on budgets has only been fully felt in the comparatively recent past. Meanwhile, the BBC has not been immune. Partly as a reaction to concern in the early 1990s that it might be losing its popular touch, partly in recognition of the more ratings-conscious and populist environment in the commercial sector, and partly to divert some resources into its new digital operations, the BBC has been every bit as rigorous in analysing its bottom lines and looking for programme 'efficiencies' (cuts) in news and current affairs.

The impact on serious current affairs throughout the industry has been severe. In the commercial sector, only Channel Four remains as a serious provider of political reporting and analysis. For nearly thirty years, ITV had a strong track record in providing some hard-hitting investigations in current affairs strands which offered a place on peak-time television for some of the most dogged and independent political reporters. As in newspapers, however, this kind of journalism is expensive, and in a ratings-conscious environment such expenditure cannot be justified by the size of audiences. With the Independent Television Commission able to do little more than deliver mild admonishments when delivery of serious programmes on commercial channels becomes inadequate, ITV and Channel Five political offerings are low-budget non-peak-time public service fig-leaves which will never sustain the kind of investment in journalistic research that used to be routine for ITV.

While the BBC maintains its commitment to peak-time current affairs, both budget and ratings pressures are also taking their toll. A combination of licence fee revenues which consistently fall behind real broadcasting costs and a series of cuts imposed on news and current affairs has meant staff reductions and squeezed budgets. Producers on *Panorama*, the BBC's flagship TV current affairs programme, insist that programmes are being made for less than they were five years ago, and are concerned about the growing pressures on staff and research time.[8] During 1999 there was a spate of incidents on factual programmes where mistakes were made as producers and researchers sought to get material on screen without making the kinds of checks that should have been routine. In one Channel Four programme on close relationships between fathers and daughters, one featured pair turned out to be a couple in a relationship; and in a BBC programme on 'sex addicts', a *Sun* reporter had great fun convincing programme-makers about her five-times-a-night 'exploits'. Although confined to documentary programmes, these and other incidents were symptomatic of a widespread sense of corners being cut and staff being pushed to their very limits to cope with the almost brutal competitiveness of the new broadcasting environment.

The impact has been felt not only on the quality of programmes, but on the nature of the material being covered. It is well known what sort of programmes bring in the punters. An analysis of how ITV current affairs programmes performed a few years ago demonstrated the importance of subject matter: while one *World in Action* exposé of the Los Angeles police force attracted 10.8 million viewers, another, identically scheduled, edition on the crisis in intensive care in British hospitals managed little more than 5.3 million. Over on *This Week*, a two-programme special on a New York mafia boss managed over 8 million for each episode compared to an audience for an in-depth investigation of the Pentagon's Star Wars programme of 4.3 million.[9] On this sort of evidence, commissioning editors under pressure from controllers or shareholders have little latitude. Cover anything involving crime, money, housing or mortgages, the royal family or noisy neighbours, and you are on safe competitive ground. Meanwhile, anything that remotely looks or sounds like politics will guarantee a ratings slump which will require explanation. At the BBC, of course, the justification is notionally an easy public service one. But even here, and particularly on BBC1, producers have recently been under pressure to change the mix of current affairs topics towards softer 'consumer' issues at the expense of serious and more difficult political stories in order to increase ratings:

> [E]ditors whose instincts lie normally with stories we would have covered five or ten years ago are pressing the button automatically and are looking over their shoulder at the sort of ratings that each programme could be expected to deliver ... subjects that would have been commissioned in the past are no longer being commissioned. And it's received wisdom, it's not disputed, everybody is concerned about ratings.[10]

Meanwhile, current affairs programmes have effectively disappeared from British commercial television as it becomes progressively more commercial and ratings-conscious. Programmes that throughout the 1970s and 1980s offered room for political journalism in peak-time commercial television have given way to drama and entertainment, while those that remain (on the edge of peak time) have moved increasingly towards ratings-led stories about crime, consumer protection and the royal family. The most recent innovation was modelled explicitly on an American programme, CBS's *60 Minutes*, featuring the viewer-friendly Trevor McDonald. Journalists in the industry have little faith in the ability of this programme to make any effort to tackle serious issues:

> '*Tonight with Trevor McDonald* is aimed entirely at the erogenous zones they think are the kind of younger, more advertising-friendly audience they want; so there's lots of video of people doing bad things, even when there's no story to tell; there's one-sided sentimental interviews; there is an obsession with crime and scary health stories. And they have a very limited range: very little foreign, no political, nothing of real significance to the country (like Northern Ireland) because these are deemed to be unpopular.'[11]

In fact, given the American model on which *Tonight* was based, it is perhaps not surprising that political content appears so impoverished and that the emphasis is on entertainment rather than information. Despite its reputation as a rare beacon of serious journalistic endeavour within the entertainment-saturated landscape of network television, systematic research on the content of *60 Minutes* suggests a rather less flattering picture. Looking at nearly 500 stories transmitted from 1990 to 1994, American journalist James Fallows calculated that 'more than one-third were celebrity profiles, entertainment-industry stories, or exposés of . . . "petty scandals" '. Meanwhile, barely a fifth concerned politics, economics, or 'any other issue of long-term national significance'.[12] British commercial television has only in the past six years been subjected to the kinds of competitive pressures that have been standard in the United States since television's inception. It has not taken long, however, for the deregulatory and free-market policies which were a legacy of the 1980s to have a material impact on the nature and volume of available political coverage. With the advent of digitalization and yet more cable and satellite channels, the situation is unlikely to improve.

There is still one area where broadcasters have apparently managed to salvage an oasis of political coverage: Sunday mornings. As we have seen, over the past few years, the Sunday morning (and lunchtime) political interview has become a staple diet of BBC television and radio, ITV and Sky News. This is partly because, in ratings terms, it is a good graveyard slot for the mainstream channels, which can sustain a worthy hour of public service broadcasting without damaging audience share; and partly because it offers individual programmes (and their producers) a chance to make headlines in Monday newspapers, whose political reporters are often short of decent material. The proliferation of such programmes illustrates the dilemmas for professional reporters trying to keep up. One of our respondents described the chaotic situation as he tried to cope with the avalanche of political interview programmes that rain down on him on a Sunday morning. He described having to keep up with four morning interview programmes, and continued:

> 'At lunchtime it's so chaotic now, it's laughable. There's BBC TV's *On the Record* and at the same time on ITV you have the *Jonathan Dimbleby Live* programme with an audience and that's followed by *Crosstalk*. At the same time as that's all going on there's *The World This Weekend* on Radio 4. I've got to juggle all of that and, with what's gone on in the morning, I have to decide what the main story of the day is – based not just on the interview programmes but a whole range of other things that have been happening, including of course the Sunday papers.'[13]

It is precisely this sort of pressure which has resulted in a much heightened obsession throughout the mass media always to be 'moving the story on'. No self-respecting journalist – political or any other – wants simply to regurgitate material which has been uncovered by a rival. Apart from professional pride, editors in a competitive business are less interested in recycling old news than demonstrating their paper or programme's ability to produce something new or different. In the course of our research, our respondents made frequent use of phrases such as 'I didn't think the story had legs'. In other words, it is an integral part of the journalistic culture that a political story which cannot be developed, at every stage in the news cycle, is not in fact a 'story'. Westminster-based broadcasters feel almost a compulsion to find new angles to existing political stories so that their output will, in the words of the trade, appear 'fresh'. In today's competitive and highly frag- mented reporting environment, to retell the same story in the same way is regarded as professional failure.

This imperative to move the story on has real consequences for the way in which politics is represented through the media. In particular, a competitive environment places a greater premium on political tension or conflict, because they are more entertaining and therefore more likely to generate interest and audiences. The temptation for all political reporters, then, is to move stories on by exaggerating or highlighting areas of conflict which in reality may be a rather insignificant part of a continuing political story. Steve Richards, while a political correspondent at the BBC, compared coverage of John Major's perennial 'leadership crisis' in 1993-5 with that of Harold Wilson's 25 years earlier when Wilson was at his most vulnerable. He concluded that

> The leadership crisis which engulfs John Major every few months is nurtured and sustained by the massive expansion in broadcasting outlets. The political inter- view . . . is now so commonplace that one feeds off another, constantly renewing a sense of political crisis and providing fresh copy for newspaper journalists.[14]

Certainly, those middle years of Major's government were characterized by a sense of complete lack of confidence within his party and a leader who was permanently teetering on the edge of political oblivion. It is unlikely that the internal strife within the Conservative Party was any greater than that within the Labour Party in the 1960s but, as Richards says, today's endless political coverage means that 'whenever a politician is in trouble, he tends to stay in trouble for much longer. In the case of a Prime Minister in a period of political turbulence, the impact can be close to fatal'.

The increasing tendency of political coverage to concentrate on areas of conflict has consequences both for fostering greater political timidity within parties and creating a more distrustful, disdaining political culture. It would be foolish to condemn an adversarial approach to political reporting, since much of real-life politics is adversarial. However, politics is at least as much about the nitty-gritty of debating and creating policy, of trying to create a better understanding of social and economic problems and searching for ways of resolving them. An emphasis on splits and personal conflict at the expense of conveying much of the other (and more constructive) work which is the lifeblood of politics does not produce a vibrant and participative political culture. The then chairman of the Conservative Party, Brian Mawhinney, made this point in February 1996 when he complained about splits between ministers, whether real or imagined, taking precedence over policy announcements. He specifically blamed the 'explosion' in the amount of political broadcasting when ministers were asked to comment on sound- bites taken out of context from earlier interviews by colleagues: 'This selective use of quotation can then be manipulated to create a wholly artificial and meaningless, but damaging, split.'[15]

A good example came two months later in April 1996 when New Labour, then in opposition and carefully building its image and public pronouncements towards the election a year later, was at great pains to emphasize that it had purged itself for good of the 'tax and spend' inclinations with which it had been associated for all its seventeen years in opposition. Its strategists were utterly convinced that the most important plank of its pre-election strategy was to reassure 'middle England' that it would not be subjected to more taxes. In the course of an interview, Labour's shadow Transport minister Clare Short said that she personally – as a comparatively highly paid politician – 'wouldn't mind paying a bit more tax'. Although she had neither commented on nor dissented from any published New Labour policy statement, her words were seized upon by a rapacious media that delighted in interpreting them as a legitimation of higher taxes. Short was immediately removed from the airwaves by New Labour's managers, even denied the opportunity of commenting on her portfolio area of transport. The reason was a paranoid fear that the media would attempt to generate policy conflict and contradictions where none existed. Hugo Young, writing in the *Guardian*, described this fear as 'understandable', and continued:

> The vultures wait to pounce on every particle of contention with an appetite they never had when Mrs Thatcher was getting the Tory Party ready to rescue Britain from the socialist nightmare. Tabloid values, played swiftly into television, kill off serious policy debate before it starts.[16]

Competition and BBC journalism

Young implicitly makes the point that in a voraciously competitive media system, even the 'public service' values of the BBC are swept along by the same journalistic instincts. Precisely this point is made by Nicholas Jones, himself a BBC political journalist who has written prolifically on the subject:

> The constant battle for readers, listeners and viewers has had a profound effect on news-gathering. . . . However much broadcasters might try to distance themselves from such influences, the excesses of the tabloids do colour their news judgement and are reflected in their treatment of politics.[17]

The point about these tabloid values is that they are relentlessly negative about politics. It a negativism with an honourable history, which makes it difficult to gainsay without qualification. Its roots are in a quite proper determination to hold politicians accountable and to demand that the development of public policy, decisions being made on the public's behalf and the spending of public money should be undertaken in the public spotlight rather than behind closed doors. The question is how that perfectly proper – indeed, democratically essential – process of scrutiny can be conducted with detached scepticism without crossing the line into derision and cynicism.

This has been a particularly vexed question for the BBC, whose political journalists are just as immersed in the competitive culture as their professional colleagues in commercial television and the press, but whose institutional and managerial aspirations are sometimes expressed differently.

The BBC's dilemma was illustrated graphically by a speech delivered by its then Director General, John Birt, in February 1995. He contrasted two traditions in covering politics, 'disputation' and 'reflection'. While accepting that disputation had 'always been an integral part of British . . . culture and society', he suggested that the balance had perhaps swung too far:

> The media today resound with acrimony, allegations of incompetence, demands for resignation. Rivalry between politicians or differences within parties are played out as a national soap opera. . . . In the era of the soundbite and the tabloid, a stray remark, a poorly judged phrase on a Sunday morning programme – a repeated evasion, a careful nuance, a finely drawn distinction – can build by Tuesday into a cacophony of disputation and a political crisis.[18]

Birt, like Hugo Young, was concerned about the real impact such contrived 'fury and hyperbole' was having on political life, suggesting that important political decisions may be adversely affected. Moreover, an approach which emphasized heat rather than light spilt over into public disillusionment with what was perceived by voters as incessant bickering at the expense of thoughtful decision-making. As the ultimate arbiter of journalistic standards in the world's most authoritative news provider, Birt wanted to set out an agenda for what he described as a greater sense of responsibility in political reporting. He emphasized the need for 'a proper balance between politics and policy' in the BBC's coverage; for ensuring that the BBC addressed long-term as well as short-term issues; for analysing issues as well as the personalities behind them; and the need to recognize that there is 'no higher democratic legitimacy than Parliament's'. In elaborating on this theme, Birt caused a stir which reverberated for several days after his speech:

> Politicians have a higher claim to speak for the people than journalists. But some journalists sometimes forget that. Reporters who pretend that answers and remedies are obvious; that everyone in the world but them is an incompetent fool; overbearing interviewers who sneer disdainfully at their interviewees. . . . all exhibit attitudes which are unattractive in a journalist, and rarely appropriate. Tone in journalism matters. A measure of humility and a little more dispassion – always in alliance with sceptical and rigorous questioning – would be worthier qualities.

Birt's problem was twofold. First, his remarks about sneering disdainfully were clearly aimed squarely at Jeremy Paxman, the much-respected presenter of *Newsnight*, whose direct and incisive questioning was not appreciated by many senior politicians. It was also not appreciated by John Birt. It was, however, held up by many journalists – and viewers – as the very model of high-quality journalistic interrogation, one which combined a thorough grasp of the issue under discussion with a determination to expose politicians who could not adequately justify a particular proposal, action or statement.

The second problem was fundamental to the BBC's ambivalent role as impartial watchdog on the one hand and publicly funded (and therefore politically vulnerable) institution on the other. Given its track record during the late 1980s and early 1990s and the fears (as discussed in Chapter 5) about a creeping culture of self-censorship, Birt's words were easily interpreted as another example of the corporation cravenly bowing to political pressure rather than an honest attempt to analyse the public service responsibilities of journalism in a competitive reporting environment. The thinly disguised personal attack on Paxman was particularly ill-advised given that 10.30 at night on a minority channel is not a time when journalism is being subjected to the downward forces of competitive pressure. However, as a blueprint for overcoming a deeply rooted cynicism in professional journalism and adopting a more democratically responsible approach, it was an interesting contribution to a debate about the democratic role of public service broadcasting.

In another consequence of competitive journalism, however, the BBC probably fares rather better. This is the pressure on all journalists to deliver stories – or angles on stories – which are more likely to generate readers or viewers. It is now received wisdom that the media are 'dumbing down', usually interpreted as a fundamental shift away from discussion of public affairs, reporting of Parliament, serious journalistic investigation and serious political commentary. Empirical evidence is not abundant, although one study of the two British 'red tops' – the *Sun* and *Daily Mirror* – established a very dramatic decline in coverage of current affairs from 1968 to 1992. In that time the proportion of editorial space given to public affairs declined in the *Daily Mirror* from 23 per cent to 8 per cent and in the *Sun* from 33 per cent to 8 per cent. In the same period, both papers' coverage of showbusiness more than doubled: from 13 per cent to 28 per cent of editorial space in the *Mirror* and from 10 per cent to 25 per cent in the *Sun*. It is likely that this proportion has risen still further in the last few years. The author of this research points to the relaunch of the *Sun* in 1969 – newly purchased by Rupert Murdoch – as the beginning of the competitive battle where the *Sun*'s editorial agenda set the pace: 'the *Sun* legitimised certain styles of journalism, particularly in the area of the private sphere. The *Sun* pursued the Royal Family, errant politicians and showbiz personalities while the *Mirror* followed some way behind.'[19]

Competition and print journalism

Similar allegations of trivialization have been levelled in recent years at the broadsheet press by commentators who recognize that the press has always been competitive but believe there has been a fundamental shift recently. The author Anthony Sampson, a member of the Scott Trust which owns the

Guardian, wrote recently that 'the frontier between qualities and popular papers has virtually disappeared'. He is clear that the root cause is the 'cut-throat contest' in which British national newspapers are engaged, in contrast to the local monopolies which dominate the American press. But, asks Sampson, 'how far does this competition provide real variety? In many ways, I believe, it has led to less choice. In particular the high ground of serious reporting, investigating and foreign coverage has been vacated.'[20] This theme was continued by Matthew Engel in the *Guardian*, who argued, on the basis of his own book on the popular press as well as on his experience as a long-standing *Guardian* reporter and columnist, that 'broadsheet newspapers have changed beyond recognition in the past ten years'. He accused broadsheets of slavishly following the tabloid agenda and attributed the change wholly to new competitive forces in the broadsheet market: the price-cutting tactics of Rupert Murdoch's *Times*, which helped it almost to double its circulation; the arrival of the *Independent* in 1986 and its attempt to attract readers from an already saturated market; and the influence of the *Daily Mail*, whose popular mid-market style and flair broadsheet editors were now trying to emulate.[21]

The kind of agenda which concerns these and other observers is one based on a mix of showbusiness personalities, royal family stories, sex scandals, entertainment and 'sleaze' stories. These have always been the staple diet of the popular press. What is new is the headline coverage given in almost every serious newspaper to stories like that of British actor Hugh Grant being caught with a prostitute in Los Angeles, or some personal crisis in the life of a famous pop star, television celebrity or sports personality – such as the decision by Spice Girl Geri Halliwell to leave the group. There is a growing sense not just of this kind of journalism replacing more serious reporting and analysis of public affairs, but of political reporting itself being degraded by an undue concentration on 'sleaze'. This is difficult territory, because one journalist's gratuitous exposé of, say, a politician's private life is another's legitimate investigation into hypocrisy and possibly corruption. While uncovering a senior cabinet minister's large and undisclosed loan from a fellow cabinet member might be a proper subject for journalistic inquiry, it is more difficult to justify some of the expansive coverage given to ministers' revelations about their bisexuality when more serious policy analysis is diminishing.

Perhaps what is most important here is the perspective of those political reporters who are caught up in the maelstrom of competition. One of Westminster's most distinguished observers is Peter Riddell, now a political columnist for *The Times* but formerly Political Editor of both *The Times* and the *Financial Times*. He observed recently:

> Increased competition, both among newspapers and broadcasting outlets, has resulted in a significant change of approach. The price war and increased competition among the broadsheets has led to a shift down market on at least the news and feature pages of many papers. The emphasis is on attracting marginal and younger

readers who are believed to be less interested in reading about 'heavy' politics – that is policy rather than personality. So while many broadsheets, if not tabloids, still carry plenty of space devoted to politics, the style has changed. An increasing number of stories are about scandal and misconduct rather than policy or procedure. Splits and disputes are exaggerated. . . . Nuances are lost.[22]

Andrew Grice, latterly of the *Sunday Times* and now of the *Independent*, reported that in his sixteen years in the House of Commons, competitive pressures in the broadsheet press had never been as intense.[23] And Colin Brown, also of the *Independent*, echoed those sentiments and described the impact on broadsheet reporters:

'It's a very old-fashioned pressure but it's to get scoops. The job of the lobby correspondent is very much to beat the competition and so we are very conscious . . . of the need to produce fresh news each day and as far as possible to have our own exclusive stories. . . . We are not here to manufacture stories [but] if the *Indy* can steal a march on everyone else then so much the better for the *Indy*. In a market where everybody is highly conscious about circulation, we have to be conscious of the need to promote the *Indy* as much as we can and I don't think there should be any apologies for that.'[24]

On tabloid newspapers, competitive pressures mean that political reporters sometimes feel they are fighting against both their editors' and their readers' prejudices against politics. Kevin Maguire, who at the time was Political Editor of the *Daily Mirror*, described how in the mid-1990s he and his colleagues had to fight off an attack from *Mirror* executives who believed that political coverage was anathema to *Mirror* readers:

'Two and a half years ago on the *Mirror*, a very senior executive told us that politics didn't sell the paper, and it would be downgraded in favour of consumer issues and so on – which of course we all thought was a tremendously good idea! It was complete and utter bollocks and a huge mistake. Politics went from page two to page thirteen. It started creeping back, and now we are back at the forefront.'[25]

While this might mean that politics on the *Mirror* has rediscovered its place at the front of the paper, it means ironically that pressure then increases to make sure that stories are new, fresh and exciting. In particular, there is more intense pressure both to come up with exclusives and to pay less attention to detail and accuracy:

'Westminster is incredibly competitive, which means that you get some of the best stories and some of the worst stories because the pressure is always on to beat your rivals and scoop them. Each national newspaper has four or more people down here which is a big investment, you know, you're talking £200,000 plus just invested in those people. And they want a return from that in terms of stories. As a result, some people cut corners, too many kites are flown and people believe what the last person told them. Gossip is picked up in the bars and it's not checked and it's run . . . people reporting ninth hand what they've learnt.'[26]

It is this combination of the age-old pressure for exclusives, the fight for survival in a declining (in newspapers) or fragmenting (in television) marketplace, and the bottom-line costs of employing full-time reporters that has made life more difficult for serious and untainted political reporting than ever before. Politicians themselves are clearly exasperated by what they see as declining standards, and in June 1996 fifty of them signed an early day motion:

> This house deplores the steep decline in serious reporting and analysis of politics and current affairs [and] notes that this decline has gathered pace in recent times, with increasing emphasis on personalities rather than politics, and on trivia rather than substance.[27]

It is axiomatic in business and industry that competition is beneficial and that without it there is stagnation, complacency and no incentive to innovate. The British national press is among the most competitive in the world, while British broadcasting has recently shaken off its protective public service mantle and is now being technologically and politically driven in the same direction. The repercussions for political reporting of these changes appear to be profoundly depressing: almost relentless cost-cutting exercises which make time-consuming investigations increasingly difficult, especially in areas assumed to have low reader or viewer potential; the evacuation of serious political current affairs by television channels forced to protect their ratings and channel share against encroachment from new commercial channels; artificial dramatization of politics to the point where even the slightest display of disagreement or tension is elevated to a political crisis; a growing emphasis on traditional tabloid stories of sex, scandal and showbiz within the broadsheet press; and pressure to cut corners and rely on hearsay rather than rigorous first-hand research in order to keep up with the incessant flow of ever-faster deadlines. As shareholders keep up their pressure to cut costs and new electronic technology offers the prospect of even more informational outlets via the Internet and cable television, it is difficult to see the twenty-first century offering anything other than more of the same. Political journalism in Britain is likely to be the poorer for it.

Notes

1. Roy Greenslade (1999) 'Who really makes the best media baron', *Guardian* G2, 8 February, pp. 8–9.
2. Matthew Engel (1996) *Tickle the Public: One Hundred Years of the Popular Press*, p. 180. London: Victor Gollancz.
3. John Curtice and Roger Jowell (1997) 'Trust in the political system', in Roger Jowell, John Curtice, Alison Park, Lindsay Brooke, Katerina Thomson and Caroline Bryson (eds) *British Social Attitudes, the 14th Report*, p. 107. Basingstoke: Ashgate Publishing. Interestingly, in their study of the 1997 general election, the authors do not find a correlation between lack of trust and voter turnout.
4. Mark Evans (1997) 'Political participation', in Patrick Dunleavy, Andrew Gamble and Iain Holliday (eds) *Developments in British Politics 5*, pp. 116–17. London: Macmillan.
5. Edward Herman and Noam Chomsky (1988) *Manufacturing Consent*, p. 17. New York: Pantheon Books.

6. Ben Bagdikian (1992) *The Media Monopoly*, p. 167. New York: Beacon Press.
7. Ian Jack (1998) 'Now for the bad news', *Guardian* (Saturday section), 8 August, p. 3.
8. This was a consistent theme in interviews with twelve current affairs producers carried out at the University of Westminster for the Campaign for Quality Television. See Steven Barnett and Emily Seymour (1999) *A Shrinking Iceberg Travelling South . . . Changing Trends in British Television*, pp. 20–43. London: University of Westminster. Producers' fears appeared to be confirmed in 2000, when *Panorama* was moved to a late-Sunday-night slot in the schedules and the number of programmes was reduced to 30 a year.
9. Steven Barnett (1992) 'Ducking the issues', *Impact*, no. 5, pp. 14–17. London: PACT.
10. Barnett and Seymour, *op. cit.*, p. 20.
11. Interview with current affairs journalist, *ibid.*
12. James Fallows (1997) *Breaking the News: How the Media Undermine American Democracy*, p. 57. New York: Vintage Books.
13. Interview, September 1998.
14. Steve Richards (1995) 'Soundbite politics', Reuter Foundation Paper no. 14, Green College, Oxford.
15. Quoted in Nicholas Jones (1997) *Campaign 97: How the General Election Was Won and Lost*, p. 140. London: Indigo.
16. Hugo Young (1996) 'A few Short words echo in the void', *Guardian*, 18 April, p. 19.
17. Nicholas Jones (1995) *Soundbites and Spin Doctors*. London: Cassell.
18. John Birt (1995) 'For good or ill? The role of the modern media'. Independent Newspapers Annual Lecture, Trinity College, Dublin, 3 February.
19. Dick Rooney (1998) 'Dynamics of the British tabloid press', *Javnost*, vol. 5, no. 3, pp. 95–107.
20. Anthony Sampson (1997) 'The crisis at the heart of our media', *British Journalism Review*, vol. 7 no. 3, pp. 42–51.
21. Matthew Engel (1996) 'Papering over the cracks', *Guardian*, 3 October, G2, pp. 2–4.
22. Peter Riddell (1999) 'A shift of power – and influence', *British Journalism Review*, vol. 10, no. 3, pp. 26–33.
23. Interview, January 1998.
24. Interview, September 1998.
25. Interview, September 1998.
26. *Ibid.*
27. Quoted in Steve Peak and Paul Fisher (1996) *The 1997 Media Guide*, p. 44. London: Fourth Estate.

CHAPTER SEVEN

The power of party machines

In opposition we made clear that communications was not something that you tagged on the end, it is part of what you do. That is something that we have tried to bring into government.[1] – Alastair Campbell

One of the most significant developments within the British political system over the past few decades has been the establishment of 'presentation' as the central philosophy not just of the practice of politics, but of its content as well. Indicative of this was a series of events at the end of 1998 and the start of 1999 which seemed to highlight the centrality of the 'spin' phenomenon to the British political process. The first came in October when *The Times* paid a very substantial sum for the serialization rights of the memoirs of Labour's polling and presentation adviser, Philip Gould.[2] The second event came in a spate of government resignations before and after Christmas – involving the then Trade and Industry secretary Peter Mandelson, the Paymaster General, Geoffrey Robinson, and Charlie Whelan, the Chief Press Officer to the Chancellor of the Exchequer. The details of the resignations are irrelevant except that they all centred round the issue of which spin doctor had been leaking what to whom. The significance of these events lies in the amount of media coverage they generated. The resignation of Whelan, for example, a medium-grade civil servant, coincided with the first day of trading of the euro; but it was Whelan and not the euro that dominated the television and radio bulletins and the next day's headlines. There can be much debate as to whether or not the editorial decisions relating to Gould and Whelan were correct in terms of traditional 'news values'; what is less contentious is the fact that both men were at the centre of Labour's communications and campaigning effort and that their respective memoirs and resignations signified important moments in the contemporary discourse of politics.

Controlling the news agenda

The centrality of the professional communicator is a relatively new development on the British side of the Atlantic.[3] Professional communicators come with a variety of expertises: media, marketing, advertising, polling, event-staging and so on. Our focus is on the activities of the corps of political press officers, now invariably known as 'spin doctors'. Their impact on the relationship between politicians and the media in recent years has been enormous and is recognition of the fact that control of the political news agenda is now acknowledged to be central to all parties' campaigning strategy. The aforementioned Philip Gould came to political campaigning from an advertising and marketing background. However, as his account of his involvement with Labour's campaigning makes clear, he recognizes how critical the news agenda, and control of it, is to modern political campaigning. He writes:

> In a campaign you must always seek to gain and keep momentum, or it will pass immediately to your opponent. Gaining momentum means dominating the news agenda, entering the news cycle at the earliest possible time, and repeatedly re-entering it, with stories and initiatives that ensure that subsequent news coverage is set on your terms. It means anticipating and pre-empting your opponent's likely manoeuvres, giving them no room to breathe, keeping them on the defensive. It means defining the political debate on your terms.[4]

The realization that control of the news agenda is central to winning elections is not new. Margaret Thatcher's key media advisers – Tim Bell and Gordon Reece – made its control, via the tabloid papers, one of their primary goals. According to Tim Bell's biographer, Mark Hollingsworth,

> Bell and Reece assiduously courted the editors of two newspapers they had singled out for special attention: Larry Lamb of the *Sun* and David English of the *Daily Mail*. Mrs Thatcher's media advisers were particularly conspicuous at the *Sun*'s offices. . . . They would drop by regularly for informal meetings with Lamb, usually in the evenings over large quantities of champagne.[5]

This view is shared by Andrew Lansley, now a Conservative front-bencher, but prior to 1997 the party's Director of Research: 'For a political party the primary objective is to control the agenda, by determining the issues of political debate.'[6]

Seeking control of the news agenda has been a constant part of Labour's campaigning perspective ever since the arrival of Peter Mandelson as Director of Communications in 1985. Speaking after the 1992 general election, Labour's former Deputy Leader Roy Hattersley said:

> 'The party which sets the agenda wins the election. Does anybody doubt that if the election had been fought around health, education or unemployment, the Labour Party would now be the government? But the election was not fought around those issues; it was fought around the issue . . . of tax in particular. That agenda was set by the Conservative Party, aided and abetted by the newspapers, with the broadcasting media as accessories after the fact.'[7]

Joy Johnson was Labour's Director of Communications in the run-up to the 1997 election. As a former news editor for the BBC at Westminster, she, more than most, appreciated that it was the news agenda that provided the campaign with its central focus. Her mission was to convince Labour that 'the party that captures the news initiative will both dominate the agenda and wrong-foot their opponents'.[8] Indeed, one of Johnson's first initiatives on assuming control of Labour's communications operations was to produce a manual, 'Driving the News Agenda', which owed much to her previous journalistic experience. In this document Johnson reveals the mechanics of such an operation: she talks of establishing a communications unit based on a newspaper or television newsroom and she sought to establish a 'story line development unit' which 'would take charge of an issue immediately it arises . . . and keep it up and running'.[9] That Johnson succeeded in creating a news-driven environment is evidenced by Philip Gould, who provides the following mini-portraits of the communications priorities of Labour's three key communications campaigners:

> Gordon Brown is constantly looking to anticipate the news and use it. He thinks that modern campaigning is news-driven or it is nothing; but the political landscape is constantly changing, always fluid – what is down now would be up soon. He thinks that you need prior momentum. There is no end point; you don't arrive; you're sailing constantly in a changing sea. Peter Mandelson can see the chaos, but wants to create order out of it; he wants defining landmarks, clearly delineated campaigns, events that can be planned and executed with consummate professionalism. He wants impeccable, perfect order. Alastair Campbell wants boldness, the audacious, unpredictable coup – the *Sun* coming out for Labour; Alan Howarth defecting [from the Conservatives].[10]

Long before Brown had entered Parliament, when still a student at university, he had identified the symbiotic relationship between politicians and the media. Writing in the student newspaper of Edinburgh University, he posed the question, 'Can the politician achieve anything?' His answer was 'I believe he can, only by first realising the limits of the possible. That his actual power is minimal, and that his real power lies as a propagandist, in providing the ideas and policies for change.'[11]

In the run-up to the 1997 election there were over 300 people working out of Labour's campaign and media headquarters at Millbank, a short walk from Parliament.[12] In addition to the teams based at the centre there were also media teams located in the offices of the party leader, deputy leader, shadow ministers, Parliament and in the party's regional offices. With Labour in government the infrastructure has remained intact but is now centrally controlled from Downing Street. The Conservatives have fallen behind in terms of the amount of resources they have devoted to media management in recent years – with numbers even in election time less than Labour's 'peacetime' media team. Nonetheless, given the sheer quantity, experience and energy of such teams on the ground, it is hardly surprising that their impact is so observable.

In a recent article Peter Riddell, now Assistant Editor (Politics) of *The Times*, who has long experience in the lobby, described how the relationship between journalists and politicians was undergoing a sea change as a result of the rise this new breed of spin doctors imported into the system by the Labour Party:

[S]pecial and media advisers to ministers have become adept in creating a sense of dependency by promising a preview of a future event or initiative, or an 'exclusive' interview to favoured reporters or papers which do not rock the boat. This has been particularly true of the leading Blairite advisers such as Alastair Campbell, Tony Blair's main press spokesman, and Charlie Whelan, Gordon Brown's personal spokesman.[13]

Tony Wright, one of the most thoughtful of Labour backbenchers, and a former lecturer in politics, believes that the changes are even more profound:

Let's start with the politicians. They like to be thought well of and want to control the message and the messengers as far as possible. There is nothing new nor even disreputable about this: it comes with the job. What is new though, is the systematic and professional way in which it is now undertaken. The wearisome jibes about spinners and sound bites to capture the modern enterprise of news management [are] central to contemporary politics. Practitioners of these black arts are increasingly the key figures in the political world. As communication flows are deliberately centralised, their authority as the source of information and opinion is further enhanced. That task is to ensure that there is a coherent and consistent message and that everyone stays 'on message' in their dealings with the media. Labour honed these skills in opposition and has carried them into government. Political communication in Britain will never be the same again.[14]

A transformed relationship

The relationship between politicians and the media at Westminster has been transformed over the past ten years. The parties' commitment to 'controlling the message' has impacted in a variety of ways, even in the apparently simple business of arranging an interview with a politician. Ten years ago a broadcaster seeking an interview with an opposition frontbencher would have gone directly to the office of the politician concerned. No self-respecting political broadcaster would have dreamt of making such a request via a party press office, unless there was some difficulty in making contact with the politician him- or herself. Today it is almost inconceivable that bids for shadow ministers and other senior politicians would not go through the relevant press officers. (The situation with ministers is somewhat different in that the activities of Whitehall press officers are not a new phenomenon, although the degree of their centralized control is.)

The undoubted effectiveness of the Labour media machine in the run-up to the 1997 election can be attributed to a ruthless efficiency which sometimes crossed the line into malign manipulation. For example, if a journalist was seeking to arrange a radio or television interview with a politician, a request might go in for Labour spokesperson 'A'. The request would be agreed and a time for the interview established. At the requisite time politician 'A' would not appear, but someone whom the Labour hierarchy deemed to be more 'on message' would. Thus the producer's dilemma: refuse to have this politician on the programme, thereby causing a row with both the spurned politician and the Labour media centre (as well as having a fairly large hole in one's programme); or accept politician 'B' and thus by default allow the Labour Party an uncomfortable degree of influence on programme content.

Another form of media manipulation would arise if an interview request had been made directly with Labour spokesperson 'A' rather than going through the press office. It would not be uncommon, after the arrangement had been made, for 'A' to call back to say, 'I've just been told that I'm not available, you'll have to phone the press office to see who's going to do the interview.' Sure enough, the press office would just happen to know that spokesperson 'B', always more reliable and acceptable to the leadership than 'A', might just be available – indeed, was already on their way to the studio.

This changed relationship in the balance of power between broadcasters and politicians has come about for three reasons. First, and most important, because Labour, the most successful of the three main parties in electoral and media terms in recent years, has sought to exercise such control as a central part of its overall communications strategy. Second, the proliferation of outlets for political news that has resulted from the rise of new television and radio channels has dramatically increased the number of 'bids' coming in for politicians and therefore created a need for some sort of systemization and prioritization. Alastair Campbell, the Prime Minister's Press Secretary, giving evidence before a House of Commons Select Committee in 1998, described this proliferation of media outlets and the consequences that flowed from it:

'[T]he scope now of the media world has changed out of all recognition, even since Bernard Ingham's[15] day. Now, in my office, we have still got the same number of people as not just Bernard Ingham, but Joe Haines[16] had. In 1979 on Radio 4, you had *Today, World at One, PM, The World Tonight, The World This Weekend*. On TV, you had 15 minutes at lunchtime, 20 minutes in the early evening and 30 minutes late on. That was 1979. Since then, you have got longer bulletins at lunchtime and early evening, you have got *Newsnight, Breakfast News, On the Record, Breakfast with Frost, Westminster Live, News 24, Sky News, Channel Four News, Powerhouse*. It's a completely different media world. Now the Prime Minister gets hundreds and hundreds and hundreds of requests for interviews from around the world every single day. He cannot meet anything remotely approaching nought point something per cent of them. All of those bids have to be dealt with, all of them have to be spoken to, and journalists who want briefings have to be briefed.'[17]

Campbell paints a gruelling picture of the Downing Street Press Office as a sort of fragile craft being buffeted on the waves of the ever-expanding media outlets (and he even omitted any mention of BBC Radio's 24-hour news channel Radio 5 Live, a voracious consumer of political interviews). This multiplication of channels and outlets, far from diminishing the power of the politicians, has enormously increased the ability of their media managers to play one outlet off against another. It has delivered enormous power into the hands of press officers to grant or deny the media access to their charges, depending on how satisfied or otherwise they might be feeling with the coverage they had received from any particular outlet. Denial of access is a relatively minor nuisance for a newspaper but for a broadcaster it is potentially disastrous, depriving the medium of the voice or picture of the central characters being reported.

The third cause of the changed relationship between broadcasters and politicians also relates to the expansion of political broadcasting over the past decade: the recruitment of an army of new researchers, reporters and producers, who, usually coming from outside the Westminster village, do not have the background in politics that their predecessors tended to have. They are, in general, younger, less experienced and with few, if any, contacts among senior politicians. The camaraderie, genuine or artificial, which exists in and around Westminster, has passed by this new breed of broadcast journalists. and hence their ability to deal with party press officers and politicians on near-to-equal terms has been very limited.

The account in Chapter 3 of political correspondents' working day would probably not markedly differ from a similar account written thirty years ago, with the major exception that their daily routine is now 'accompanied' by a corresponding routine by the parties' media departments. For like the news organizations, they have their own daily editorial meeting where they look at the issues that have arisen so far and are expected to come up later. At these meetings they plan their own media initiatives and work out how to respond to opposition moves and to other news developments. This sort of operation is what one might anticipate during an election period but is now a permanent feature of the political scene, a very tangible example of the 'permanent campaign' which now characterizes Labour's political strategy. Alastair Campbell described the way the Labour government started its daily media operations as follows:

> 'In terms of the structure of the day Peter Mandelson[18] chairs a meeting at nine o'clock at which you have representatives from Number 10, from the Foreign Office, from John Prescott's office,[19] from the Treasury, from Ann Taylor's office,[20] from the Chief Whip's office, from the Cabinet Office and from the Labour Party. At those we do two things. We go through a media brief which goes through basically a four- or five-page digest of everything that is in the newspapers and running on the programmes that morning. It gives the headlines on the six-thirty news, the seven o'clock news, et cetera. We see if there are any problems arising out of that. We see if there is anything we did yesterday that we might have done differently and we talk about it. We then go on to today's agenda, as we see it, of the things that we are going to be promoting.'[21]

On the day that Campbell was describing this process he was also able to boast of his, and his team's, success in establishing that their agenda was dominating that day's news. On no fewer than four occasions he told the parliamentary select committee before which he was appearing that a new education initiative that the government had launched that morning was dominating all the radio and television bulletins – ironically until Campbell himself started giving evidence, when he succeeded in knocking this initiative off the top of the bulletins.

In fact, for many of Campbell's team their 'day' might well have begun the previous night in negotiating with Radio 4's *Today* programme, or other broadcasting outlets, about the 'terms of engagement' for the upcoming morning's interviews. These terms might include the placing of the interview in the programme, the order in which other interviewees might be heard and the actual area of questioning. This discussion might well have ranged over what could not be covered as well as what could; too much intransigence from a radio or TV producer will sometimes result in the press officer saying, 'I think my man might find it rather difficult to fit in this particular interview.'

Once their daily meetings are concluded, the press officers move into proactive mode. This involves contacting journalists with story lines and ideas, writing and distributing press releases, chatting in the Commons lobby and elsewhere with correspondents, lunching them, seeking them out in the press gallery and, all the time, keeping a wary eye on the broadcast media, the *Evening Standard* and the Press Association wires.

One way of analysing the impact of party media operations on the production of political news is to break their interventions down into 'above' and 'below-the-line' forms of activity. 'Above-the-line' activities are those overt initiatives taken by media managers that, in very simple terms, an 'old-fashioned' press officer would have happily engaged in. 'Below-the-line' activities are those now associated with the term 'spin doctor'; they are usually covert and are as much about strategy and tactics as imparting information.

Above-the-line activities

Government/party announcements

Government or party announcements can be routine, something planned for many weeks or even months ahead; or they can be more immediate, contrived to show either the government or an opposition party reacting to a new development. There are many ways such announcements can be made. Both governments and opposition parties distribute press releases, organize press conferences, issue statements to the Press Association, make announcements via interviews or speeches, stage events or 'let it be known' by a press officer or an adviser or the politician concerned having a discreet word with one or several journalists. But governments have other means as well. They can:

- make ministerial statements in the House either directly or via a Private Notice Question;

- respond to a 'planted' written or oral question from an MP;
- make a statement to a Commons committee;
- use a ministerial broadcast to the nation; or
- simply publish an announcement in the *London Gazette*.[22]

This huge range of devices means that, on the one hand, political journalists receive a constant stream of stories every day – on an 'average' day the table in the reporters' gallery at the House of Commons groans under the weight of between 30 and 40 press releases. Equally, it means that government in particular, and the parties to a lesser extent, can slip out official announcements that they do not wish to have subjected to public scrutiny in a way that the most sharp-eyed journalist could easily miss. With such a plethora of material swirling around, journalists can find it rewarding to follow up announcements that have been drawn to their attention by a 'friendly' press officer; but in the process they can easily miss those announcements that for one reason or another no one has mentioned to them.

Reacting to government/party announcements: rebuttal and 'prebuttal'

During the course of the political day the opposition parties in particular, but also the government, seek to react as rapidly as possible to moves from the other side. They can react in virtually all the ways listed above, apart from using the parliamentary devices, but the commonest form of reaction is to wait for or to seek out the opportunity of putting their case directly. They can do this either by talking with journalists in the lobby or – if the intention is to break into that same day's news cycle – by seeking out a broadcast interview, making contact with the Press Association or speaking with the London *Evening Standard* (which, through its four editions, provides a flow of breaking stories that reach journalists and politicians alike).

Prior to the 1997 General Election Labour had this technique down to a fine art with what the party called its 'rapid rebuttal unit'. Very much based on the experience of Bill Clinton's successful US presidential campaign in 1992, Labour had taken to heart the Democrats' maxim 'speed kills'. In other words, the best way to kill off an opposition story was to rebut it as rapidly as possibly, preferably in the same news cycle. Philip Gould described the 'philosophy' behind Labour's famed 'rapid rebuttal unit', at Millbank:

> Campaigning is about speed. The British electorate, like almost every electorate in the world, is subject to a continual assault by news. . . . Any political assertion, however false, can spread through this media jungle with the speed of a panther. The world of politics is littered with assertions that are untrue, but are believed to be true because they were not effectively answered. An unrebutted lie becomes accepted as the truth. You must always rebut a political attack if leaving it unanswered will harm you. And you must do it instantly, within minutes at best, within hours at worst, and with a defence supported by facts.[23]

In the twelve months leading up to the 1997 election Labour's rebuttal operation was in full swing. If the government or the Conservative Party called a press conference to launch their latest policy initiative or to mount some new attack on Labour, Labour would frequently announce its own press conference for an hour later in order to rebut the claims. Sometimes their rebuttal was even swifter; if they had word in advance of the Tory onslaught, it would not be uncommon, at the conclusion of the Conservative press conference, to be greeted by Labour Party workers proffering press releases containing Labour's rebuttal to what had just been announced. It could be even quicker still. Journalists listening to the address to the Conservative Party Conference at Bournemouth in 1995 being given by the then Chancellor of the Exchequer, Kenneth Clarke, found themselves being paged with rebuttal 'soundbites' from the office of the Shadow Chancellor, Gordon Brown, even before Clarke had sat down. And quicker still: a 'prebuttal' statement might be issued in advance of the original attack even being made.

Publicizing interviews and speeches

In the recent past, Friday afternoons were the time when the thud of party press releases could be heard hitting newsdesks across Westminster as ministers' or shadow ministers' weekend words were pre-released to the media. Frequently these releases referred to speeches being made by ministers, or their shadows, in their constituencies, and they often involved a 'speech to party workers' (the assiduous journalist turning up to the constituency would usually find that although the meeting might have been taking place, the minister was strangely absent). The 'speech' was merely a device to enable the politicians' words to reach the public in what looked like a report of an event but was in fact a report of a press release.

Much of the impact of these weekend speeches has been blunted by the rise of the Sunday political shows, a political communications practice imported from the United States. At the last count, the following heavyweights now square up to political guests on a Sunday morning: on the BBC Sir David Frost and John Humphrys, on ITV Alastair Stewart and Jonathan Dimbleby, on Sky News Adam Boulton, plus regional political shows on both the BBC and ITV. In addition, Radio 4 and Radio 5 Live both have political interview slots.

The effect of this plethora of talk is that much political interchange takes place in the Sunday television and radio studios. There has been some debate about the significance of these programmes (see Chapter 3), and they certainly provide much-needed copy for political correspondents on duty on a Sunday and looking for material. Because they have relatively few distractions, there is a great deal of scope for poring over the words of the politicians in microscopic detail. The 'spinning' by the parties is immense. A good example of this was late in 1997 when the Prime Minister, Tony Blair, was due to appear on the BBC to respond to questions about the relationship between Labour's change of policy on banning tobacco sponsorship for motor racing and a donation of £1 million from one of the sport's leading figures. The Sunday morning papers, a full twelve hours before the interview had taken place, were telling their readers on the basis of 'authoritative sources' what Tony Blair was likely to say to his interviewer.

Reacting to interviews or speeches

The same process applies to policy announcements and initiatives, where the media become intermediaries in a political dialogue. A minister gives an interview on the *'Today'* programme for example; the shadow minister then picks this up, either directly from *Today* or from the Press Association or the *Evening Standard*, and puts out his or her own counter-statement and perhaps gives an interview to the lunchtime broadcast media. This in turn provokes a counter-reaction from the government, whose response can be heard on the *PM* programme on Radio 4 or the early evening television bulletins. The opposition then responds in time for the main news bulletins or the late-night television programme *Newsnight*. Thus within one news cycle an issue can be aired on four occasions, with politicians and media acting in a collusive relationship to 'move the story on'.

Reacting to breaking news events (and 'staying on-message')

Keeping up to date with a breaking story requires a high degree of organization and flexibility. Thus, a politician turning up to a news organization about one story has to be prepared to take questions on a later breaking story; and to do this the politician has to be kept informed of both the story itself and his or her own party's (possibly changing) line. During the 1997 election a Labour candidate who had agreed to be interviewed was asked to comment on a breaking story. Before agreeing to do so the candidate called his party's press office for approval and for basic information about the story; then he, and the reporter, had to wait until headquarters had given him the go-ahead and sent him a pager message containing the requisite 'line'. Such an 'on-message' reaction is possible only in an era when mobile communications technology has become commonplace. Equally, of course, it is only the advent of virtually instantaneous electronic journalism that has necessitated such a speed of response.

Labour in government has taken the whole process one stage further with a transcript of what Alastair Campbell, the Prime Minister's Press Secretary, has told the 11 a.m. lobby meeting, now being transmitted to Labour's media department at Millbank and then faxed or e-mailed to all Labour MPs within 30 minutes of the end of the briefing. Thus armed, all backbenchers should be fully 'up to speed' with the government's policy on the latest breaking stories should they find themselves in front of a microphone or camera later in the day.[24]

Below the line

Spinning

The basic operation of the spin doctor can be characterized more as a process than as an event. It can be seen in its purest form at party conferences and particularly around the leader's speech. At the Labour conference, for example, the speech is delivered on the Tuesday afternoon. The spinning will begin with the Sunday papers being offered a few morsels of what might be in the speech and what its main themes might be (in fact, some of these will be deliberate false trails, some attempts at pre-emption or kite-flying – see below.) These reports will be followed up by the Monday newspapers whose correspondents will have received a few more titbits. A few hours before the speech itself there will be a formal session when the leader's Press Secretary will go through the speech, pointing out its themes and highlighting particular announcements and even phrases or soundbites. During the speech itself odd moments of spin will occur – press officers will sidle up to journalists and say, for example, 'That went down well.' After the speech the spin will continue in a semi-formal debriefing, as journalists huddle around the lead spin doctor, followed by one-to-one briefings. In this operation the broadcasters are crucial because the immediate 'post-match analysis' by politicians, TV pundits and conference delegates is watched avidly by journalists and press officers alike, and forms the vital backdrop to the way in which the speech is subsequently described.[25]

A classic example of the spin doctor's role – and an illustration of the difference between a traditional press officer and the modern spin doctor – came at Labour's conference in 1994, Tony Blair's first as party leader. Blair used his speech to announce his intention to abandon Labour's commitment to public ownership – Clause 4 in the party constitution, which for many party members was a symbolic expression of Labour's continuing commitment to socialism. The leadership was concerned that if news of this move leaked out, some delegates might start heckling during the speech – a calamitous prospect. Hence two precautions were taken. First, when the speech was distributed to journalists, a few minutes before Blair began speaking, the last three pages of the speech were missing: journalists were told that it was not yet ready, and the missing pages were distributed a few minutes before Blair reached that portion of the speech. Second, even the announcement itself was couched in such coded language that virtually no one in the hall (including journalists who had the text in front of them) appreciated its full import until a team of spin doctors fanned out from Labour's press office, after the speech, to spell out precisely what the leader had been saying. While press officers deal in what the politician will say or has just said, the spin doctor's stock-in-trade is what he or she actually meant.

Attempting to set the day's news agenda

Politicians see setting the political news agenda as central to their objectives, and as part of the overall strategy of leaving little to chance. Parties spend much time during election campaigns, but also increasingly in so-called 'peacetime' between elections, attempting to control the media's news agenda. Five months before the 1997 election, Labour planned to announce that the party was committing itself to not increasing income tax rates for the lifetime of the next parliament. Labour was anxious that this story should come out at a time of its choosing and on its own terms. Too little notice of a breaking story can leave journalists scrambling to catch up and consequently unable or unwilling to give the story the greatest impact. Too much notice gives both journalists and opposition politicians a chance to jump on the bandwagon and feed journalists substantial 'rebuttal material'. To achieve maximum value, timing is all.

Labour's handling of the tax announcement[26] was a classic of its kind. Journalists' appetites were whetted the day before with the suggestion that the shadow Chancellor, Gordon Brown, was to make an announcement about Labour's spending plans, but no mention was made of income tax. So journalists were primed to expect a story the following day but not primed in sufficient detail to enable them, either through their own efforts or with the assistance of the opposition parties, to 'get their retaliation in first'. In the words of BBC Political Correspondent Nick Jones: 'In retrospect, one could not but admire the sheer effrontery with which Labour eventually succeeded in marshalling the news media into greeting Brown's promise [of no tax rises] with such uncritical acclaim.'[27] The 'effrontery' that Jones admired was the ruse used by Brown's press spokesman, Charlie Whelan, to gain the coverage. He had arranged for Brown to be interviewed by the influential *Today* programme and ensured that the rest of the media knew that Brown was making an appearance. Ostensibly Brown had agreed to be interviewed about his spending plans, but Whelan suggested to the programme's presenter, James Naughtie, that at the end of the interview he might slip in a question about Labour's tax plans. This he did and Brown, on cue, revealed his policy.

He did not wish to make his tax plans the centrepiece of the interview for three reasons. First, he did not wish to give the programme the chance to invite his Conservative opposite number onto the programme to respond immediately and thus diminish the impact. Second, he wanted to save the substantive discussion about his plans to follow the lunchtime speech he was due to make that day, which was the ostensible reason for the interview in the first place (he thus gave himself the opportunity of gaining a new round of media interviews as a result of the story developing during the day). And finally, the surprise element of the announcement would reinforce its impact and make it appear to be an even bigger story than it was (although in fact Labour press officers had been preparing correspondents for such an announcement in the preceding months). The operation worked and the tax announcement achieved maximum attention, setting the agenda not just on the day in question but for the next few days as well.

Driving the news agenda

Driving the agenda differs from setting the agenda in that it involves a sustained campaign of driving the news in a particular direction over a period of time. During the summer of 1996, for example, the Labour Party demonstrated its ability to drive the news agenda in its own chosen direction. The summer is always a difficult time for politicians; there is a certain inevitability that a major crisis will break just at the moment when every senior figure is unavailable. Sometimes, however, crises can be made to break. During the summer of 1996 Labour decided to ensure that the two-pronged attack it had undertaken against the Conservative government's privatization measures stayed on track. The two prongs were, first, the apparent failures of the newly privatized utilities to deliver high-quality services to their customers; and second, the large bonuses being paid to senior management and shareholders at the same time as customers' bills were continuing to rise. Labour took advantage of the relative paucity of news during the summer months by feeding the media with a series of stories about the mishaps in areas such as the water supply or the rail service while at the same time drawing attention to the latest large pay-out to the directors of these companies.

Joy Johnson, who was at the time Labour's Director of Communications, described the process in an internal Labour Party document:

> We seized the agenda at the start of the summer with water privatisation and so Labour became the party of the consumer. The discussion in newsrooms was not about 'water meters being a good ideas to preserve water' but instead it was about 'how the privatised water companies were not investing to stop leakages'. It quickly became apparent that we could capitalise on anti-privatisation sentiments so we targeted the *Today* newspaper, a paper known to have concerns about privatisation. By giving the political journalist a series of exclusive angles on various privatisations, he ran a story-a-day to help us in our specific campaign against British Rail privatisation.[28]

Firebreaking: distracting attention away from an uncomfortable story

A firebreak is a deliberately constructed diversion to take journalists off the scent of an embarrassing story which seems to have developed a momentum of its own. A classic of the genre was successfully invoked by Labour in the summer of 1997 when the *News of the World*, briefly returning to its traditional role of attacking rather than supporting Labour, revealed that the Foreign Secretary, Robin Cook, was engaged in a long-term relationship with his secretary. As a result of the newspaper's disclosure, Cook, allegedly under pressure from Alastair Campbell,[29] announced that he was going to leave his wife. Labour's spin team reacted with speed. Apart from ensuring that Cook confronted his own personal crisis, the party's media machine 'created' two other stories to take journalists' eyes off the difficulties of the Foreign Secretary. First, to coincide with the *News of the World*'s story about Robin Cook, the *Sunday Times*'s later editions carried a sensational story reporting that MI6 was investigating the former Governor of Hong Kong, Chris Patten, over alleged breaches of the Official Secrets Act in connection with his recent book about his time in Hong Kong. That Sunday morning Labour's Peter Mandelson, who was then in charge of government presentation, was due to appear on BBC Radio's *The World This Weekend*. It was later revealed that he had told one of the BBC's political correspondents that, if asked on air, he would confirm the Patten story.[30] Mandelson was indeed asked and did indeed confirm it but, just to make sure that the journalistic sand was sufficiently kicked in the eyes of the journalists, he also tossed into the interview the fact that the government was thinking about reprieving the royal yacht, *Britannia*, which was due to be scrapped. The results are to be seen on the front pages of the following day's broadsheets. Not a single one led on the Robin Cook story, a result of what one member of the Downing Street press team described as 'a fantastic operation'.[31]

Another example came late in 1998 when the Labour government was hit by its first major scandal, involving the then Secretary of State for Wales, Ron Davies, who was forced to resign after being involved in a bizarre incident in south London which newspapers hinted might be linked to either casual gay sex or drug use or both. Three days after the story first broke, and with no signs of its being eased off the front pages, the government suddenly brought forward a statement on its plans to reform the welfare system. The *Independent* newspaper quoted a Conservative Party adviser explaining what the government was trying to achieve: 'It's a straight damage-limitation exercise. They [the government] always tell the Opposition when a statement is about to be made, but this time they've told us nothing. It's obviously a smokescreen.'[32]

Stoking the fire

Stoking the fire is the mirror image of 'firebreaking': finding material to keep an opponent's awkward story running. During the years of John Major's continuing difficulties with his own party over Europe, it was relatively easy for Labour spin doctors to keep this particular story running. However, another example where this tactic has been used with some success by the Conservatives was over continuing allegations that Labour's then Paymaster General, Geoffrey Robinson, who had ministerial responsibility for plugging loopholes in the tax system, was himself involved in activities that the Conservatives claimed involved tax avoidance. A well-orchestrated campaign involving both selected newspapers and opposition frontbenchers succeeded in keeping this story running for many months at the end of 1997 and during the first half of 1998. These allegations undermined the Paymaster General's position to such an extent that speculation that the Prime Minister would be forced to move him out of that position continued unabated. At the end of the year he resigned, ostensibly over a secret loan he had made to Peter Mandelson, but he himself said in his resignation statement that the main reason for his resignation was the constant allegations and media pressure.

Building up a personality

The classic case of building up a personality was the exercise undertaken by Peter Mandelson, as Labour's Director of Communications, when he set out to build up the media profiles of two young Labour MPs: Tony Blair and Gordon Brown (subsequently Prime Minister and Chancellor of the Exchequer respectively). This he did by putting their names forward to radio and television producers who were in search of interviewees, drawing journalists' attention to press releases that these two had issued, and by briefing journalists on a regular basis that these two MPs were politicians to watch. He was undoubtedly right, but part of the reason why they were 'politicians to watch' was the very media operation conveying this message.

Undermining a personality

The opposite activity is, in a way, even easier to undertake. The classic operation in this mould was the undermining of Conservative cabinet ministers who had fallen out of favour with the then Prime Minister Margaret Thatcher. In one notorious example in 1986 the Prime Minister's Press Secretary, Bernard Ingham, sought to dismiss comments by the then cabinet minister John Biffen, who had had the temerity to suggest that Mrs Thatcher might not be Prime Minister in perpetuity. Ingham told the lobby that Biffen was 'a semi-detached member of the government', a phrase reprinted in virtually every newspaper the following morning. The result was devastating. As Ingham's biographer, Robert Harris, observes,

> Biffen was left to twist in the wind for another year, before eventually being cut down and deposited on the back-benches two days after the 1987 General Election. ... Biffen was an awful warning to his colleagues of the penalty for lese-majesty.[33]

Identical allegations have been levelled at Alastair Campbell during much of his tenure as Tony Blair's official spokesman, culminating in a particularly venomous attack in July 2000 by one of the Labour Party's wealthiest and most long-standing supporters, the novelist Ken Follett. His accusations of 'cowardice' aimed at the Prime Minister for not directly confronting ministers whose careers might be in decline failed to appreciate the relatively long history of such practices.

Pre-empting

A classic example of pre-emption occurred towards the end of 1998 when, following the resignation of Ron Davies, the *News of the World* informed the Agriculture Secretary, Nick Brown, that it was intending to run a story alleging that he was gay. Brown, instead of waiting for the newspaper story to appear, issued a statement to all newspapers confirming that he was indeed gay. This did not stop the *News of the World* from running its own story but ensured that it remained a 'one-day wonder', and Brown's ministerial career was unaffected.

Kite-flying and managing expectations

In a kite-flying operation, governments or parties use the media to float proposals in order to test or manipulate reaction. Kite-flying can most obviously be witnessed in the weeks leading up to the announcement of the Chancellor's Budget statement. A week before the Conservatives' Budget in 1995, a story appeared in the *Observer* claiming that the Chancellor was going to introduce a windfall profits tax on the public utilities.[34] It was, as subsequent events revealed, untrue (although the Labour government did introduce such a tax two years later). It was, however, a typical case of either kite-flying or pre-empting. In other words, the story either emanated from the Chancellor's office, which was keen to gauge reaction to the introduction of such a tax, or came from those opposed to such a tax who wanted to create a level of opposition which would dissuade the Chancellor from introducing such a measure.

Similarly, expectations are carefully managed around Budget time when the Chancellor lets it be known that this year the Budget will be particularly problematic. Judicious leaks appear at almost regular intervals as to the extent to which the Chancellor is going to have to raise taxes. Everyone expects the worst and then, amazingly, a little extra is found and the Budget is hailed as a triumph.

Milking a story

Milking a story is the technique by which a government or party extracts as much positive media coverage as possible. Soon after Labour gained power in 1997, the Speaker of the House of Commons started to complain about the fact that announcements that ought to be made to the House of Commons were being trailed many days in advance in the newspapers and on the broadcast media. Andrew Grice, now Political Editor of the *Independent*, described how the process felt from his side of the parliamentary gallery:

> 'Spin doctors are very clever. They work out a strategy for presenting a White Paper and then they say, "right, we'll give it a little bit to the Sundays, another bit to the Mondays, and then another bit to the *Today* programme on Wednesday when we launch the White Paper", and there's not much the journalist can do about that sort of operation.'[35]

Throwing out the bodies

All governments have items of bad news that they need to disseminate into the public arena without attracting too much attention. Every day dozens of press releases and written parliamentary answers are distributed to the parliamentary press gallery. It is not a difficult matter simply to put out a press release either at a very busy time when journalists are distracted by other stories, or conversely at a very quiet time (e.g. during a parliamentary recess) when few journalists are around. An alternative scenario was described by a former Whitehall Head of Information. The informant explained that when a major 'royal' story broke, the prime minister's press secretary would immediately phone all government press offices suggesting that now was a good time to put out any awkward announcements they had been storing up, safe in the knowledge that the media's attention would be distracted by the latest chapter in the ongoing saga of the Windsors.[36]

A more recent example came during the Labour Party conference of 1998, when, much to the annoyance of the Labour leadership, four left-wingers were elected to the party's National Executive. The announcement of the election result was due to be made on the Tuesday of conference week but was suddenly rushed forward to the Sunday. At the same time a story was leaked that Gordon Brown, in his speech the following day, would say that he had no ambitions to replace Tony Blair as party leader. It was the Brown story that dominated the Sunday evening bulletins and the following day's newspapers.

There are times when even the most assiduous spin doctor is unable to lay his or her hands on a convenient royal scandal in order to camouflage an item of bad news. This is where the technique of 'laundering' comes in useful – a phrase first used by Sir Angus Maude, who was Paymaster General in the first Thatcher government, and responsible for presentation of government policy.[37] This involves finding a piece of good news that can be released at the same time as bad news; if the timing and presentation are right, the good news will succeed in relegating the bad news to the inside pages.

The 'white commonwealth'

The 'white commonwealth' is the name given to a favoured group of correspondents who receive special treatment and access, above and beyond that available to other political correspondents. The name originated under Harold Wilson and his Press Secretary, Joe Haines, who during the Rhodesia crisis developed a concept of trusted journalistic friends who could be relied on to provide favourable coverage and helpful advice. BBC Political Correspondent Nick Jones described the workings of the 'white commonwealth' under the regime of Margaret Thatcher's Press Secretary, Bernard Ingham, and how it tended to allow Ingham a relatively 'easy ride' in the lobby briefings:

> Under Ingham's no-nonsense regime those reporters who were employed by newspapers sympathetic to the government had no wish to sour relations by challenging him needlessly. They knew they had every chance of speaking to him by phone after the organised briefing, when they might find it easier to obtain the information they wanted.[38]

Jones makes similar claims about the existence of a 'white commonwealth' under both John Major's and Tony Blair's regime.[39]

Bullying and intimidation

Of course, the notion of any privileged 'in-group' requires an 'out-group' which is less privileged. Reporters 'out of the loop' can find themselves not just excluded from sources of information but also openly bullied. Bernard Ingham was the first to be charged with such behaviour but under Labour the tactic has been developed almost into an art form. Even when Labour was in opposition, dealing with its media machine posed something of a quandary for the political journalist. Accept the line, the spokesperson and the story and all would be well: the journalist would get his or her interviewees, a regular drip-feed of minor exclusives and the sense of being on the inside. However, sign up for the 'awkward squad' and the result would be interview bids turned down, access to breaking stories denied and no flow of exclusives. Although this is a dilemma that constantly faces all journalists in any sort of lobby, it has become particularly acute with New Labour because the 'game' is played with an unprecedented degree of bitterness and brutality.

Intimidation of individual reporters and media institutions has been a part of the political scene for many years. The attempts, frequently successful, to bully and intimidate the BBC have been well documented and stretch from Winston Churchill during the General Strike to Tony Blair and the 1998 bombing of Iraq. However, the bullying has become particularly personal in recent years. In the run-up to the 1997 general election the Political Editor of the *Daily Telegraph*, George Jones, often bore the brunt of attacks from Labour's media managers. He hit back with a front-page story headed 'Why I Will Not Be Intimidated':

> . . . it is another example of a campaign of intimidation by Mr Mandelson against journalists who write anything with which they do not agree or which is critical of Labour. Mr Mandelson seems to believe that if he can embarrass people in front of their colleagues they will be less likely to write anything that can be seen as anti-Labour. On one earlier occasion, Mr Mandelson warned me that The Telegraph would not get any more Labour stories if one of my staff continued writing reports which he did not like.[40]

There are, no doubt, other techniques and devices not described here which political parties have developed over the past ten years in order to control the production of political news. Our argument is that with the growing levels of sophistication and resources being invested in these techniques, and with levels of investment in journalism marching inexorably in the other direction, politicians have an increasing measure of success in controlling the news agenda. Furthermore, not content with keeping a tight rein over their own representatives and party machinery, governments are also seeking more rigorous control over information emerging from the Whitehall machine.

Notes

1. Alastair Campbell at the Select Committee on Public Administration, 23 June 1998.
2. Philip Gould (1998) *The Unfinished Revolution: How the Modernisers Saved the Labour Party*. London: Little, Brown.
3. See David Kavanagh (1995) *Election Campaigning: The New Marketing of Politics*. Oxford: Blackwell, for a description of the beginnings of modern campaigning.
4. Gould, *op. cit.*, p. 294.
5. Mark Hollingsworth (1997) *The Ultimate Spin Doctor: The Life and Fast Times of Tim Bell*, p. 70. London: Coronet.
6. Andrew Lansley, unpublished lecture given at the London School of Economics, November 1994.
7. Roy Hattersley (1993) speaking at 'The Westminster Consultation'. Unpublished transcript, Goldsmiths College, London.
8. Joy Johnson (1995) 'Driving the news agenda'. Unpublished Labour Party internal document.
9. *Ibid.*
10. Gould, *op. cit.*, p. 260.
11. *Student*, 18 May 1971. Quoted in Paul Routledge (1998) *Gordon Brown: The Biography*, p. 50. London: Pocket Books.
12. Gould, *op. cit.*, p. 308.
13. Peter Riddell (1998) 'The media and Parliament', in Jean Seaton (ed.) *Politics and the Media: Harlots and Prerogatives at the Turn of the Millennium*. Oxford: Blackwell.
14. P. Wright (1998) 'Inside the whale', in Seaton, *op. cit.*, p. 20.
15. Chief Press Secretary to Margaret Thatcher, 1979–90.
16. Chief Press Secretary to Harold Wilson, 1969–76.
17. Alastair Campbell, evidence to Select Committee on Public Administration, 23 June 1998.
18. At the time Peter Mandelson was Minister without Portfolio with special responsibility for the effective presentation of the government.
19. At the time, Deputy Prime Minister.
20. At the time, Leader of the House of Commons – the government's legislative business manager.
21. Alastair Campbell, evidence to Select Committee on Public Administration, 23 June 1998.
22. This is the official publication of Her Majesty's Government.
23. Gould, *op. cit.*, p. 295.
24. Quoted in Nicholas Jones (1999) *Sultans of Spin: The Media and the New Labour Government*, p. 284. London: Gollancz.
25. *Ibid.*
26. For a detailed account, see Nicholas Jones (1997) *How the General Election was Won and Lost*, pp. 91–6, London: Indigo Press.
27. *Ibid.*, p. 91.
28. Johnson, *op. cit.*
29. According to the account by Cook's biographer, John Kampfner (*Robin Cook*, London: Gollancz, 1998) Campbell told Cook 'clarity in news management was the only way they were going to get out of it. Cook interpreted "clarity" as [meaning that] he should make a choice one way or another' (p. 154). But Derek Draper, a former aide to Peter Mandelson, says Campbell was more direct: 'Campbell was typically blunt with Cook', he writes; 'if he didn't want the story to run for days he had to decide whether to stay with his wife or leave' (Derek Draper (1997) *Blair's 100 Days*, p. 209. London: Faber & Faber).
30. Draper, *op. cit.*, p. 210.
31. Kampfner, *op. cit.*, p. 158.
32. *Independent*, 29 October 1998.
33. See Robert Harris (1994) *The Media Trilogy: Good and Faithful Servant*, p. 783. London: Faber & Faber.

34. *Observer*, 26 November 1995.
35. Interview, January 1998.
36. Conversation with Gaber.
37. Quoted in Michael Cockerell, Peter Hennessey and David Walker (1984) *Sources Close to the Prime Minister: Inside the Hidden World of the News Manipulators*, p. 50. London: Macmillan.
38. Jones (1997) *op. cit.*, p. 90.
39. *Ibid.*, pp. 116 and 168.
40. *Daily Telegraph*, 21 November 1998.

CHAPTER EIGHT

Controlling the Whitehall machine

One of the most profound impacts of Labour on the political communications process has been on the work of the government's own information machine – a massive and unwieldy body that was in urgent need of modernization. Just after the 1997 election one of Labour's senior media managers spoke of the difficulties he and his team, fresh from their election triumph, were having in working with the Government Information Service (GIS): 'What they [Whitehall press officers] can't seem to grasp is that communications is not an after-thought to our policy. It's central to the mission of New Labour.'[1] He believed his complaint to be perfectly legitimate, but behind this 'philosophy' of media first and message second lie dangerous implications for the democratic process - particularly since that philosophy has now become enshrined as part of the government's new information policy.[2] However, it would have been difficult not to feel some sympathy for this Labour media manager, for prior to May 1997 the GIS had been in a state of profound malaise. Many information officers did not come from journalistic or public relations backgrounds – indeed, such backgrounds, it was often argued, could be a disadvantage since they were liable to make the information officer 'too sympathetic to the press'.[3] Essentially, many saw their job as being largely to protect their ministers from the unwelcome intrusions of the media rather than acting as intermediaries between the media and their political masters. Overall, journalists working in Westminster recount a sense of dealing with a group of people with little understanding of the processes of journalism and a poor sense of public accountability or responsibility. Indeed, it was not just journalists who were appalled. Andrew Grice, then of the *Sunday Times*, recalled how new Labour ministers reacted to their first dealings with government press officers, after their experiences of dealing with Labour's media operation at Millbank: 'Some ministers were appalled to discover that press officers didn't have mobile phones and pagers and around-the-clock cover despite the 24-hour media village in which we live.'[4]

Immediately after the election, journalists found dealing with Whitehall even more problematic than before. Not only did some government press officers continue their old patterns of evasion and procrastination, but to this was added ignorance of what government was actually thinking and planning, and a real sense of anxiety about their individual and collective futures. Added to this sense of isolation and uncertainty was the presence of a veritable army of special advisers, all closer to the new ministers and to the media than the Whitehall information officers. One example will suffice. On the day of the new government's first Queen's Speech – at the start of the new Parliament - an over-anxious press officer was pressing a television producer at Westminster for a list of questions for his minister, who was due to appear on an upcoming live programme. The press officer was implicitly saying that unless the questions were forthcoming the interview would be in jeopardy. While this exchange was in train, the minister, unaccompanied by any press officer, arrived at the studio and, oblivious to the threats being made by his press officer, told the producer that he was ready and willing to be interviewed without any reference to the questions that might or might not be awaiting him.[5]

The relationship between Labour's media managers and the Whitehall information machine was probably even more problematic than that between Whitehall and the media. One example took place at the time of Labour's first Queen's Speech, which is followed by several days of debate. Following one slightly awkward question-and-answer exchange involving the Prime Minister, it was decided that a member of the government would have to make an impromptu tour of the broadcasters' studios to make reassuring noises on air. The media manager, the minister and the head of his press office all gathered in the minister's office to discuss the 'line' the minister should take. The minister asked if he could see a video recording of the relevant exchange in the Commons. He was told that this was not possible as it would have to be ordered from the Central Office of Information, and that this usually took three days. Aghast, the Labour media manager immediately arranged for somebody at Labour's media headquarters to play the relevant exchange down the phone to the minister. The Whitehall press officer, feeling somewhat humiliated, thought he had discovered a fatal weakness in the Labour operation and pointed out that by playing the extract down the phone they had had to stop the machine and thereby missed recording some of the debate. It had not occurred to this press officer that there might be more than one video recorder at Millbank Tower. 'It was that at moment', the media manager observed, 'that I realized why the government had been performing so badly in the media over the past year or so. They had no idea of what was going on - and it showed.'[6]

When the Blair government first came to power there was a great deal of alarm about what appeared to be the sudden demise of a large number of heads of information in a number of government departments; depending on how one counted, the number who left ranged from six to ten.[7] While some resigned, apparently for better jobs elsewhere, others were clearly eased out by ministers and special advisers who were less than impressed with their performance. A process of 'Millbankization' had begun - that is, substituting the operational norms, values and behaviour of Labour's election-winning media machine for the more staid methods of operation of the Government Information Service.

But one could also argue that a long-overdue and much-needed process of democratization and modernization was taking place. For the first time, senior posts in the GIS were being externally advertised, and although some of the posts still went to career civil servants, it was now clear that knowledge and/or experience of journalism was no longer an automatic disqualification from holding such posts.

But the process of 'Millbankization' did not just involve broadening the recruitment net for senior civil servants in the information field. From an early stage the Prime Minister's Press Secretary, Alastair Campbell, made clear the level of his own dissatisfaction with the Whitehall media machine. In the autumn of 1997 he circulated a letter to all Whitehall press officers telling them in blunt terms to 'raise their game'[8] and, at much the same time, the Prime Minister set up a task force under Robin Mountfield, the Permanent Secretary at the Office of Public Service, to identify how the Government Information Service might best benefit from exposure to the information and communication techniques that Labour had developed in opposition.

The results of that review, the so-called Mountfield Report,[9] published in November 1997, began with the ringing declaration that 'The effective communication and explanation of policy and decisions should not be an after-thought, but an integral part of a democratic Government's duty to govern with consent.'[10] The report identified three 'issues at stake', namely:

(i) the strategic coherence and co-ordination of the Government's main policy messages;
(ii) the need for closer integration of policy and its communication throughout the policy process; and
(iii) effectiveness, within the established conventions, in a fast-changing media world.[11]

These three issues provide the framework for understanding how the government's media operation now functions. Millbank as a centre of operations has been replaced by the Downing Street press office, which operates as a strategic centre in a far more significant way than in the past. The timing and content of all major government announcements are now controlled by the Prime Minister's press office. The timing of the release of White Papers, official statements of government intent, is now a decision for Downing Street. This control is exercised via the Strategic Communications Unit. The establishment of such a unit, whose function is to oversee the government's overall media strategy, was one of the key recommendations of the Mountfield Report. In launching the unit in January 1998, the Prime Minister said, 'The aim of the unit is to make sure events are scheduled, launched and followed through to maintain impact and to convey the central story and themes of the Government in all its communications.'[12]

It could be argued that the Prime Minister, in setting out so clearly his information goals, was simply formalizing what previous prime ministers had aspired to. Margaret Thatcher's legendary alter ego, Sir Bernard Ingham, admitted to similar ambitions. He once described his job as seeking 'to ensure that the government's communications orchestra is seen and heard to be playing from one score in tune and in time'.[13] Alastair Campbell, in giving evidence to the Select Committee on Public Administration, was keen to play down the extent to which these changes had impacted adversely on the Whitehall information machine. He told the committee:

'I know there have been a number of changes and that has obviously been unfortunate not just for the individuals concerned, but also its effect on morale. From my own perspective, I think that we, coming in from opposition, have been able to bring improvements to the way that the GIS is working, but likewise I think we have been able to learn things from the way that they have done things as well. One of the real boons of the last 15 months is that the transition has worked extremely well.'[14]

However, the question remains: is the Blair government's management of information qualitatively different from that practised by its predecessors? According to Jill Rutter, until 1997 Head of the Treasury Press Office, it is. For, she claims, the government's media managers have realized just how valuable a resource 'information' can be. She told a meeting of the Social Market Foundation think tank:

'Once the news is out – in a speech or an official release - it is a free good, but unrealized information is a valuable commodity. The genius of the government's news managers is to recognize and exploit that fact and use it to create a long-term dependency relationship. The Whitehall version of *Trainspotting*.'[15]

It might be argued that Rutter had a particular score to settle. She had after all been eased out of her position, none too subtly, by Gordon Brown's personal press secretary, Charlie Whelan (himself later to be a victim in an even more brutal way).[16] But in her speech she accepted that there was a need for change, admitting that she herself had been 'appalled by the lazy, cynical habits adopted by many of the . . . old-timers in GIS'. She then went on to express her concern that under the new regime the crucial distinction between party media relations and government media relations was becoming blurred: 'It is one thing for parties to spin and manipulate – but should governments do it . . . at taxpayers' expense?', she asked. And she went on to warn about what she saw as the very real dangers that lay ahead. The Mountfield Report had described one of the roles of the GIS as exploiting 'the natural advantages of incumbency'. Rutter warned that we could be on the slippery path of turning the Government Information Service into 'a powerful machine to secure the permanent advantages of incumbency'. And she called for a new code of conduct on the handling of government information, 'to protect the press and through the press the public's right to what is, after all, our information – in today's speak the people's information – in a way that enhances, rather than undermines, the quality of our democracy'.[17]

Rutter articulated the changing demands that Labour in government has been imposing on the Whitehall information machine. These demands result from a very different concept of the relationship between policy formation and information flow that is at the heart of the Labour government. That difference can be characterized as one in which:

- lines of control are highly centralized on Downing Street;
- all communications have to be seen to be contributing to the government's key messages;
- the concept of 'joined-up government' requires much greater liaison between departments; and
- ministers' special advisers play a central role in media relations.

This new environment has been particular stressful for government press officers because it contains conflicting centrifugal and centripetal forces. There are strong centralizing forces emanating from a government which sees communications as a core activity and to this end ensures that the Downing Street press office and Strategic Communications Unit are seen as virtually omnipresent. In the words of Jill Rutter,

> 'We're facing a greater demand from the media and a greater expectation from this Government. Throw in an expectation from the centre that we undertake planning and are being strategic and we just can't be dealing with the here and now.'[18]

This apparent inability to meet the demands of Downing Street has led to the growth of a spirit of mutual hostility. Alastair Campbell believes that the Whitehall information machine is an inferior operation, and this has resulted in Whitehall press officers believing that no matter what they do, Downing Street will never be satisfied. As one interviewee described it:

> 'Number 10 makes the crunch decisions, that's the new factor. When I first started working here you never got a call from Downing Street. Now the SCU [the Strategic Communications Unit] calls five or six times a day checking up with us. Every time you meet an expectation they raise the game. You get the impression that they are not satisfied with how we are doing our job.'[19]

Not only does Downing Street seek to keep a close eye on the activities of Whitehall press offices in terms of monitoring their activities, it also requires that all communications should be seen to reflect the government's key messages (these include 'governing for the many, not the few', 'a modernizing government' and, of course, 'education, education, education'). This in turn can create situations in which members of the GIS (now renamed The Government Information and Communication Service, GICS) feel they are being asked to cross the invisible line between government and party information.

Another factor adding to the centralizing pressures on press officers is the government's oft-trumpeted concept of 'joined-up government' - the notion that major initiatives cross traditional departmental boundaries and therefore have to be co-ordinated centrally. It makes sense in theory but in practice involves significantly more work for government information officers, as one explained: 'Joined-up government means winding into our work the overarching themes of New Labour. It's a requirement, not an option, and liaising with other departments is more time-consuming and cumbersome.'[20]

Yet despite seeking to transform their ways of working in order to comply with these new pressures, Whitehall press officers are, in general, demoralized. There is a belief that no matter how much they change, the Prime Minister and his entourage will remain dissatisfied. One Whitehall press officer expressed it thus:

> 'We work very hard but there's a feeling coming out of Number 10 that we're not measuring up. I thought we were coming to understand each other – our political and policy initiatives were beginning to mesh – but it's not being reflected from Number 10.'[21]

However, there are also contradictory decentralizing tendencies at work. For at the same time as Whitehall press officers have been struggling, apparently unsuccessfully, to assuage the government's centralizing information tendencies, they have found themselves equally pressurized to increase the profile and activities of their own departments and ministers, sometimes in ways that directly conflict with the requirements of Downing Street.

Virtually all new ministers and secretaries of state arrived in Whitehall with a highly developed sense of the importance of presentation. Most Labour ministers attribute Labour's electoral success to the primacy they gave to communications, and it is a primacy they intend to maintain in office. In addition, ministers are acutely aware that their own political trajectories are highly dependent on their own media profiles. They almost all take an intense interest in how they are perceived by the media to be doing their job. Labour's commitment to increasing the public visibility of the actions of government is graphically demonstrated by the huge increase in the number of press releases flowing from Whitehall which between 1995 and 1998 rose from 5,712 a year to 10,303.

As one example of this trend one can look at the environment, an area which the new government identified as a high priority in terms of presentation. In 1995 the ministries covered by the Department of the Environment, Transport and the Regions (created by Labour when it came into office) issued 1,283 releases. By 1998 this figure was up to 4,718 – an increase of 368 per cent (almost 20 press releases every working day).

Ministers have been reinforced in their view of the importance of the media by the special advisers that most have imported from opposition into government. There are more than 60 special advisers, twice the number that operated under the previous government. They have, in general, come from a culture in which the first consideration was invariably 'How's it going to play?' – a reference to the media in general and Labour's targets, such as the *Sun* and the *Daily Mail*, in particular. One such special adviser commented:

> 'My minister has to keep his eye on the policy – both the big picture and the details. It's my job to work out the ramifications of these policy choices, not just in terms of the politicians but also in terms of the media.'[22]

This second-guessing of media reaction to policy initiatives can cause problems for the departmental information officers. For not only do they have to be looking strategically at how the policy pronouncement should be handled and making their own calculations about likely media reaction, they also have to calculate how the minister's private office might be making the same calculations, and perhaps coming to different conclusions. A Whitehall press officer pointed out the consequences:

> 'It's sometimes safer to keep your head down and leave the planning until the last minute if the alternative is risking an almighty row with the special adviser, who, after seeing your plans for a media launch, might decide that you've got it all wrong.'[23]

And it is not just a process of second-guessing the minister or his or her special adviser. Government press officers are constantly made aware of the all-seeing, all-hearing Downing Street machine which seems to monitor their every move or moves they fail to make. One press officer articulated the feeling that many media initiatives coming out of Downing Street were based on little more than whim: 'Alastair Campbell or Tony Blair read a few articles or see a TV programme and they start to worry that the government's messages are not getting over. They get a vague idea that something must be done.'[24]

But pressure is coming, not just in terms of the expectations of what press officers do, but also in terms of how they do it. And in this area neutral observers might agree that Downing Street in general, and Alastair Campbell in particular, were making demands that cannot possibly be met by the sort of people who make up the backbone of the GICS. In the memorandum quoted earlier in which Campbell called on the service to 'raise its game', he set out in some detail what his expectations were: 'Decide your headlines, sell your story and if you disagree with what is being written argue your case.'[25] This degree of media control might be within the grasp of Campbell and other experienced, and highly talented, operators, but to suggest that every one of Whitehall's 1,500-plus press officers has the ability to deliver this sort of control to their political masters is hardly realistic. However, it does betray how Downing Street sees its relations with the press. Despite protestations to the contrary from the lobby, the view from Downing Street is that the political correspondents are unproblematic and that other departments should seek to gain the same degree of ascendancy over their specialist journalists as Downing Street clearly feels it has over the lobby. Indeed, there are occasions when, according to one senior Whitehall press officer, they are pressed by Downing Street to let them release a particularly problematic story because they believed that 'their control of the lobby would achieve the best possible coverage'.[26]

Despite the evident problems, even the most recalcitrant of government press officers recognizes that the outcome of this new, highly disciplined approach to media dissemination has had its positive side. The media coverage that the Labour government has received, sleaze and scandals aside, was for its first three years in power mostly positive. And the co-ordination between government departments, the central responsibility of the Strategic Communications Unit, improved significantly. As one press officer recalled, 'Under the previous government you found yourself making announcements on the same day as other departments – it's now much better.'[27]

Unfortunately, there has been a price to pay for this none too subtle concentration on communication and presentation. More than any government in British history, New Labour has attracted a reputation for sacrificing substance in the rush to present a coherent and positive image. Ironically for a government which has presided over an uninterrupted economic boom and which has, as some observers have commented, behaved like a true Labour government in shifting more public expenditure into education, health and helping the genuinely needy, the Prime Minister and most of his cabinet colleagues are saddled with reputations as 'spin merchants'. There is no question that it has attempted to exercise a greater degree of communications control over the machinery of government than any previous government. Nor is there much question that some reform was long overdue. In tandem with New Labour's techniques for dealing with political journalists, however, these reforms have in mythology and in practice given the government yet more power and influence over the journalistic process.

Notes

1. Private conversation.
2. See 'The Mountfield Report: A Summary': the working group on the Government Information Service (GIS), chaired by Sir Robin Mountfield. London: Cabinet Office, 1997.
3. Private conversation.
4. Interview, January 1998.
5. Based on Gaber's personal experience.
6. Private conversation.
7. The actual number is a matter of conjecture; Jonathan Haslam, who was head of Information at the Department for Education and Employment, resigned, ostensibly for a higher-paying job in the City, but only days after a bruising encounter with one of his ministers about the role of Whitehall press officers in relation to party propaganda.
8. Press reports, 2 October 1997.
9. Referred to above.
10. The Mountfield Report, *op. cit.*, para. 2.
11. *Ibid.*, para. 3.
12. Press reports.
13. Bernard Ingham (1995) 'The awkward art of reconciliation', in Peter Jones (ed.) *Party, Parliament and Personality*, p. 45. London: Routledge.
14. Alastair Campbell, evidence to Select Committee on Public Administration, 23 June 1998.
15. Jill Rutter, speech to Social Market Foundation, London, 5 December 1997.
16. Whelan was forced to resign at the start of 1999 following allegations that he had been behind revelations about Peter Mandelson's financial affairs that led to the latter's resignation from government.
17. Rutter, *op. cit.*
18. *Ibid.*
19. The following quotations are based on a series of confidential interviews with senior Whitehall information officers, conducted by Ivor Gaber between January and March 1999.

20. *Ibid.*
21. *Ibid.*
22. Private conversation with Special Adviser, October 1998.
23. Interview with senior Whitehall information officers, January–March 1999.
24. *Ibid.*
25. Quoted in *Financial Times*, 2 October 1997.
26. Interview with senior Whitehall information officers, January–March 1999.
27. *Ibid.*

CHAPTER NINE

The changing reporting culture

'Westminster works on nudges, winks and a quiet word here and so on. And it's not the best way of working. They pull you in and try and make you part of the club. They also try and get away with flying kites, only for you to discover that there's no bloody rope on the end of them.'[1] – Kevin Maguire, Political Correspondent

Politicians' ability to gain more control of both the broadcasters' and the newspapers' news agendas have been enhanced by changes in the practice of political journalism that have created conditions which astute politicians, and their media managers, have been able to exploit. In Chapter One we referred to 'structural changes within the media industries that are tending to militate against a reporting culture which is thoughtful and challenging, and towards one which is rushed and conformist'. BBC political correspondent Nick Jones makes this point forcefully:

> By the late 1980's increased competition in broadcasting had led to changing patterns in reporting. Each news programme was striving to establish a separate and distinct identity. News summaries were being revised and rewritten from one hour to the next. More often than not, the top political story of the day was also being treated differently throughout the day by the main news bulletins. This required extensive reworking and repackaging between the lunchtime, teatime and main evening news programmes.[2]

Westminster reporting, like much else in contemporary journalism, has been industrialized – more stories being produced for more outlets at ever greater speed. The modus operandi of the average political reporter has changed radically in the past few years, with perhaps the most significant change being the virtual disappearance of reporters from their three most visible Westminster hunting grounds: the press gallery, the House of Commons lobby and the Downing Street briefings. Paradoxically, this diminution has occurred at the same time as an increase in the number of reporters based at Westminster.

We have already noted in Chapter 3 the decline in the reporting of the actual proceeding of Parliament. This decline has affected the behaviour of both reporters and politicians. In the not-too-distant past, reporters used to keep a sharp eye on the annunciators: television monitors located around Parliament which visually 'announced' the name of the current speaker and the subject of his or her intervention. The appearance of certain names on the monitor – in the 1970s Enoch Powell for the Conservatives or Michael Foot on the Labour side – was enough to create a rush of reporters into the gallery to see and hear their contributions. Now the annunciators are all but ignored. The names of MPs, ministers and backbenchers flash on and off the screen with barely a desultory glance from journalists around the Palace.

Journalists have lost interest in the immediate events in the chamber for three main reasons. First, if a potentially newsworthy event has taken place inside the chamber, because of the televising of Parliament a recording of the event can relatively easily be obtained from one of the broadcasting outlets. For broadcasting journalists, the proceedings of the House are being monitored in the broadcasting studios across the road from Parliament – because journalists working on the daily radio and television programmes that summarize the proceedings of the House monitor all interventions and alert their news desks if something happens that requires following up. Indeed, frequently the most common way in which journalists in the House learn about a development in the chamber is when one of the TV or radio correspondents receives a pager message asking them to gain reaction to an event that neither they, nor in all likelihood any potential interviewee, had witnessed. Their print colleagues receive similar tip-offs from their news-desks, but usually via the more cumbersome route of the intervention being reported by the Press Association.

The second reason for this lack of interest in the chamber is that the business conducted on the floor of the House is now deemed far less newsworthy. This is a consequence of five major trends:

- The large majorities that Conservative and Labour governments have enjoyed over much of the past twenty years have meant that the result of most parliamentary deliberations has been well known in advance.
- The spirit of backbench independence, which used to be a feature of the House of Commons, has all but vanished. Its virtual disappearance is partly due to the much tighter discipline now imposed on MPs by party whips but also results from the arrival in the House of a new breed of career-politicians whose sights are clearly set on gaining a foothold on the first rungs of the ministerial ladder and who are therefore temperamentally that much less interested in rebellion.
- The influence of the select committees has grown, which has diverted some media attention away from the business transacted on the floor of the House.
- The 1997 Labour government, following a trend first set by the Thatcher governments of the 1980s, manifested a decreasing lack of interest in and respect for the House of Commons. (The then Speaker, Betty Boothroyd, complained on numerous occasions that most major announcements were being made in the studios of the *Today* programme first and in the chamber second – a practice that shows little sign of diminishing.)
- Finally, much decision-making has been devolved from the House of Commons, either to a whole raft of so-called 'Next Steps' agencies by the

Conservative government or to the devolved assemblies in Scotland and Wales or to the European Commission in Brussels.

The third reason for the decline in journalists' interest in the chamber emanates from the behaviour of politicians themselves. Because the political conflict is now predominantly played out in the media, the ability to speak in public and to sway an audience by the power of oratory has been all but lost. The vast majority of MPs and parliamentary candidates now eschew the public meeting. During both the 1992 and 1997 campaigns Labour Party headquarters actively advised candidates against holding public meetings, on the grounds of their being a waste of campaigning time and possibly even counter-productive in that they might provide opponents with a platform. It is indicative of this change that Labour by-election candidates receive training in television and radio interview techniques and in how to conduct themselves at press conferences but not in public speaking skills.

The second journalistic hunting ground which is in decline is the lobby of the House of Commons. This used to be the focal point of contact between journalists and politicians. It was where reaction to breaking stories could be gleaned, where new stories would begin life and where experienced journalists could sniff the political air, to gain a sense of the way the wind was blowing on both the front and back benches. Andrew Roth, author of *Parliamentary Profiles*, who has reported from Westminster since 1953, in an article entitled 'The Lobby's Dying Gasps?' wrote:

> These days I put a figurative mourning band on my arm as I walk from the Commons Central Lobby to the once-bustling Members' Lobby. As I pass through the swinging doors, all that greet my ageing eyes are one or two Lobby journalists and perhaps an MP or two before me at the Vote Office's open window, also collecting their *Hansards* and other documents. Talking to Commons civil servants, colleagues still in the Lobby and veteran MPs, either still in the Commons, or 'retired' into the Lords, there is one main topic. We all cry on each other's shoulders, figuratively speaking, about the 'death of Parliament' and with it, the 'dying gasps' of the Lobby system of Parliamentary journalists.[3]

Even though there are over 200 journalists who have access to the lobby it is rare to see more than half dozen there at any one time – apart from times of high political drama. One such example came late in 1998 when the leader of the Opposition, William Hague, revealed during Prime Minister's Questions that Tony Blair had been trying to strike a deal with the leader of the Conservative peers, Lord Cranbourne, about reform of the House of Lords. Hague declared that he was opposed to any such arrangement (and a few hours later sacked Lord Cranbourne). When Prime Mininster's Question Time ended that day, the lobby buzzed. Reporters, after cursorily listening to the normal briefings from Labour and Conservative spin doctors, scurried down to the lobby of the House of Commons in order to gain reaction from MPs to the sensational events that had just unravelled.

Andrew Roth sees the arrival in the House, after the 1997 election, of a new breed of government backbencher as the main reason for the decline in the importance of the lobby. He bemoans their lack of independence:

> Except for a few ageing deviants ... the 'new' Labour Party has swallowed wholesale the doctrine that the British public does not like divided parties. And that all MPs' disagreements should be taken up with the Whips, Ministers or aired perhaps in the Parliamentary Labour Party. But *never* in public, and particularly not in Parliament. In Parliament, Labour MPs who want to keep their seats and perhaps even be promoted should restrict themselves to adoring stooge questions.[4]

That is not to argue that reporters are having less contact with MPs, only that the current crop of government backbenchers is seen as a particularly unhelpful source. The presence in the House of this new breed of career-orientated politicians, particularly in the Labour intake of 1997, has resulted in a noticeable decrease in the daily interchange between journalists and politicians. A new Labour MP told one of the authors, after a brief exchange in the lobby of the House of Commons, that he really ought not to prolong the conversation since he had been instructed by the whips' office to report all contacts he had with journalists.[5] Another aspect of this change in culture has been the trend for backbench MPs to be replaced in the lobby by spin doctors. This is a relatively new development and one to which the House of Commons authorities have turned a blind eye. They too have implicitly recognized that there has been a change in the mode of interaction between politicians and journalists, and that this has required ever more active gaggles of spin doctors making themselves available in the lobby to act as intermediaries.

This lack of face-to-face contact between journalists and politicians is partly compensated for by an increasing use of other means of communication. This is a relatively new development, made possible by new technology: mobile phones, pagers and e-mail. In the past, if a journalist wanted to make contact with an MP he might have phoned the MP's office, would usually have received no reply and would then be redirected to 'members' messages'. The message would then be taken down, by hand, and left in a pigeon-hole in the members' lobby. It would reach the relevant MP either by means of the Member checking his or her pigeon-hole, or as a result of one of Parliament's frock-coated messengers spotting the relevant MP in a committee room or elsewhere, and passing on the message. In other words, the chances of a journalist making contact with an MP in time to meet a deadline were remote.

However, pagers, mobile phones and e-mail have transformed the situation. Eager reporters and MPs can now find each other with relative ease. There is another advantage to this arrangement in that conversations can now take place in complete confidence. At a time when party managers are ever more watchful of who is saying what to whom, the sanctity of a private phone can prove irresistible. This has made life easier for all concerned (apart from the whips), but has reduced the time for which MPs and journalists need to 'loiter' in the lobby in the hope of 'doing business'. Thus, although the process of getting a quote from an MP is considerably easier, para-doxically, because of this reduction in the amount of face-to-face contact, something has been lost in the nature of the relationship between the politician and the reporter; less mutual trust is engendered and the quality of political reporting inevitably suffers.[6] At the same time, it is worth bearing in mind the strictures of Peter Riddell, a former Political Editor of *The Times* and the *Financial Times*:

> There is, of course, a danger for anyone over 50 writing about a decline in his or her field of journalism. Usually, when the rose-tinted spectacles are removed, the past looks a good deal less alluring. There was never a golden era of political journal-ism. ... The leading practitioners of 30 years ago, such as David Wood of *The Times*, could appear self-satisfied, arrogant, aloof and often not that informative about what was happening outside the conventional world of Westminster politics.[7]

There are other ways in which the nature of the exchange between journalists and politicians has changed in recent years. More and more business is conducted not just on the phone, but over lunch and away from Westminster. In an environment in which information is tightly controlled by the govern-ment and the parties' press offices, ministers and Opposition frontbenchers who do wish to exchange information with journalists now feel safer in doing so away from the prying eyes of their minders. It is not always foolproof. Before the 1997 election the Conservative government's Defence Secretary, Michael Portillo, found himself in some political difficulty after voicing to two BBC correspondents some mildly anti-government thoughts. The brief-ing took place in a restaurant some way from Westminster but not sufficiently far away that the threesome were not recognized and that fact reported – resulting in subsequent embarrassment for the minister and journalists when the contents of that lunch were reported and attributed to 'friends of Michael Portillo'.

A final reason for the absence of journalists from the lobby is quite simply pressures of time. Ironically, the introduction of new technology in the national press has in many cases actually shortened deadlines. Trevor Kava-nagh, the Political Editor of the *Sun*, describes a 'a rather nerve-racking climax in the mid-afternoon'[8] as the time approaches when he has to begin filing his stories. Given that the Commons does not begin to sit on most days until 2.30 in the afternoon, there is a very small window of opportunity for political correspondents to gather their material and then file their copy.

The Head of News for the BBC at Westminster in the mid-1990s, Joy Johnson, was constantly enjoining those of her political correspondents who were not working on specific stories to spend time in the lobby. Johnson has said, 'I want them to be there because that's where the stories are that interest me – not the press releases and the daily briefings.'[9] It was the normal currency of Westminster that time spent in the lobby chatting to MPs, even just chatting with other correspondents, was never time wasted. Even if no specific stories were encountered, new contacts were established, old contacts reinforced and the face of the lobby correspondent became known to more and more MPs. But since the 1997 election, trips to the lobby have tended to be made for a specific purpose. It is not that political correspondents have become lazy, merely that they are realists who have to ration their time in such a way as to maximize the journalistic return.

The third 'hunting ground' of the political journalist that has been relatively deserted of late has been the twice-daily Downing Street press briefings, referred to in the earlier chapters. The average attendance at morning briefing is usually not much more than 20 and the attendance for the late afternoon briefing hovers between 20 and 30 – barely 10 per cent of the members of the lobby. There are several reasons for this decline. First, with the increased output of the broadcasting media, more and more political information is being made available outside the official briefings. Most major announcements are prefigured, not just by ministerial appearances on the *Today* programme, but frequently days before, by means of a series of judicious leaks. In addition, the Press Association, Sky News, Radio 5 Live, ITN News and BBC News 24 ensure that if any major story breaks at the briefing, it will be conveyed to their live audiences almost before the lobby correspondents have walked from Downing Street back to the Commons press gallery. Then there is the informal pooling whereby journalists, acting as they often do to help each other, brief colleagues who have not been able to attend the lobby as to what might or might not have transpired there. In the BBC such contact is institutionalized. Tannoy announcements call those free from immediate duties to hear a report back from one of the BBC journalists who had attended the Downing Street briefing.

A second reason for the decline in attendance at the lobby is the increasing trend by senior members of the lobby to telephone the Downing Street press office, either before or after the formal briefing, to gain a 'steer' as to the day's major news stories. Broadcasters are the most prone to do this, often claiming that they require information in advance of the briefing to meet their ever-encroaching deadlines. There is also a tendency for the more senior political correspondents to hold back from questioning in the briefing itself in the hope of receiving a more tempting private morsel later. Jackie Ashley, political editor of the *New Statesman*, recently described this phenomenon:

> More significant than the lobby meetings are the phone calls and briefings which take place outside. A group of lobby members, often comprising John Sergeant of the BBC, Mike Brunson of ITN, Elinor Goodman of *Channel 4 News* and Phil Webster of *The Times*, will sometimes wait behind after the lobby meeting for a private huddle with [Alastair] Campbell. It's then, and in private phone calls, that much of the valuable 'feeding' takes place. Campbell's savaging of the reporting of John Simpson [of the BBC] from Kosovo was the product of one such 'huddle'. This, too, is a tradition. In the trade it is known, bitterly by those excluded, as 'the white commonwealth'.[10]

A final reason for the low attendance at these briefings is that more and more political news is being signposted well in advance. It is rare these days that Downing Street uses the lobby briefings to announce a major initiative. Media managers now have the process of squeezing the maximum coverage out of a single announcement down to a fine art. The bare outlines of the new initiative might first of all be leaked to the Sunday newspaper as part of the normal Friday afternoon briefing; these stories will then be followed up by daily journalists working on Sunday, looking for stories for Monday's; and on the morning of the announcement a minister might appear on the *Today* programme on BBC Radio 4 to give a few more details, so that by the time the minister stands up in the House to make the announcement there is precious little that is new. This process ensures maximum good-news coverage for the government, but also deters journalists from attending the briefing since they think they have a pretty good idea of the upcoming political agenda.

Patrick Wintour, Political Correspondent of the *Observer*, has seen the process at work and has learnt almost to appreciate the spin doctors' expertise:

> 'We have image-makers who are, I think, much more sophisticated at handling the news, manipulating the news, than any of their predecessors. . . . They've learnt how they can run stories two or three times over: first in a Sunday newspaper, then it will appear Sunday for Monday, then it will appear on the day it actually happens. . . . And they know that they will be able to get their own spin on a story because the journalist won't have any other take on it except from what's coming from Downing Street – that then shapes the way some particular issue or some presentation is seen. So by the day the actual announcement is made, it's old hat, old news.'[11]

The impact of the Internet on political reporting is still relatively new, and, given the centralized nature of the Westminster news village, its impact at the moment is still more limited than it is in other areas. Nonetheless, it cannot be discounted. Electronic access to government and party press releases and reports is affecting the need that news organizations have previously felt to have a physical presence at Westminster. The ability to access and search Hansard, the daily report of parliamentary proceedings, has also made an impact. Select committees, which now carry full transcripts of their sessions online, are attracting more coverage, although for daily newspapers journalists' attendance at committees is still required. At the 1997 General Election, political campaigning on the Internet was still very much in its infancy, but it is anticipated that at the next election Web campaigning will play a more significant role.

However, it is not just changes in media technology that are affecting the nature of political journalism. One of the most significant changes that has been taking place across the United Kingdom has been the growing tendency, in the broadcasting sector, to seek to report and analyse politics from a non-Westminster stance. Since the advent of devolution in Scotland and Wales in 1998, the broadcasters have been seeking to increase the amount of time they devote to Scottish and Welsh politics from Edinburgh and Cardiff, respectively. In one sense this has had a profound effect on the conduct of political journalism; in another sense, very little has changed. The profound change has been, unsurprisingly, the view of politics as seen from Edinburgh and Cardiff. The Scottish and Welsh political correspondents of the BBC and ITV are now based in their respective capitals rather than at Westminster and their major focus of political coverage is now their own devolved assemblies. The same is true for the daily newspapers based in Edinburgh and Cardiff.[12]

The creation of the new assemblies in Scotland and Wales might have had a profound impact on political reporting in those parts of the United Kingdom but their impact on the political reporting establishment in London has been negligible. This is partly because the Westminster Parliament itself has virtually chosen to ignore the existence of these new assemblies. For despite the presence of these new democratically elected assemblies, Westminster still has Scottish and Welsh question times, Scottish and Welsh select committees and Scottish and Welsh grand committees.[13] Futhermore, Westminster is still the base for the political editors and there is little mileage in their seeking to downplay the importance of Westminster and consequently their own standing within their organizations. This situation is reflected in the fact that despite intensive pressures at the time of the creation of the Scottish Parliament in 1998, the BBC has resisted all pressures, both inside and outside the Corporation, for the creation of a dedicated news bulletin for Scotland in the early evening – the so-called 'Scottish Six'. In the following year, as the groundswell of dissatisfaction continued to grow, the BBC launched an opt-out for Scotland, not on its main channel at 6 p.m. but on the minority BBC2 channel at 11 p.m., when viewers in Scotland were forced to leave the daily network news programme *Newsnight* for their own fifteen-minute offering – a compromise that pleased no one. In July 2000, after months of recrimination, the BBC decided to abandon the opt-out.

Just as the nature of politicians has changed in the past decade, so has the nature of political correspondents. There are now more women in the lobby, a change that has been (almost) universally welcomed. However, there has been another, almost opposite, change taking place with the growth of what Peter Riddell calls a 'laddish' culture: 'Remarkably few seem interested in the latest political books or biographies, except where they provide a good story.'[14] Riddell goes on to argue that this new type of lobby journalist, through either cause or effect, is part of a shift in the culture of political journalism – a shift that has seen the emphasis move away from reporting about issues to stories about scandal and misconduct. Jackie Ashley, writing in the *New Statesman*, draws an interesting parallel between changes in the Labour Party and changes in the lobby:

> The new and the old co-exist unhappily. The running joke through lobby meetings
> is that there is Old Lobby – the likes of Jones of the *Telegraph*, Robin Oakley of the
> BBC, John Deans of the *Mail* and Michael White of the *Guardian*. And then there's

New Lobby – young turks such as George Pascoe Watson of the *Sun* and Patrick Hennessy of the *Standard*, who talk a language, shared with Alastair Campbell, incomprehensible to those not immersed in football culture: 'Christ, amazed you could hold your head up this morning'; ' Yeah, Shearer's complete crap . . . you lot are finished', and so on. New Lobby, the theory goes, are a gang of boozy lads about town, with no understanding of political theory but a sharp line in over-selling a story and no compunction about muddying the facts. Old Lobby, they retort, are worthy old farts, who have no idea what their readers are interested in, wouldn't recognise a real story if it hit them on the nose and are far too nice to politicians.[15]

The case for the defence of this new style of journalism was put by Kevin Maguire. He attributed this new style of political journalism to the decline of deference in society in general and in the Commons press gallery in particular:

'I think [there's been a] decline in deference generally . . . papers and journalists now put the boot into politicians, whereas in the past they wouldn't. You might doff your cap at the Prime Minister, but you'd never really go after them. But now, no compunction. I believe in adversarial journalism and they are all up there for grabs, they set themselves up, they put themselves up for public office, get all the trappings; well, they are there to be knocked down when things go wrong as well.'[16]

It is perhaps no coincidence that one of Maguire's closest friends is not a fellow member of the lobby but Charlie Whelan, the former Press Secretary to Gordon Brown. Whelan also fits into the 'laddish' stereotype and, arguably, he himself belongs to a new breed of political press officers who have grown up, the mirror image of the 'laddish' political correspondents – both perhaps finding they have more in common with each other than with the older generation of political correspondents and press officers who played the 'game' within a set of rules that seem increasingly outdated. The journalist Paul Routledge, a close friend of Whelan, described him as a member of the 'bad lad tendency'.[17] Certainly older political correspondents have not taken kindly to the spread of attempts at bullying and intimidation, accompanied by crude language, which now characterizes many of the exchanges that take place on a daily basis between journalists and press officers.

Notes

1. Interview, September 1999. Maguire now works for the *Guardian*.
2. Nicholas Jones (1996) *Soundbites and Spin Doctors*, p. 129. London: Indigo Press.
3. Andrew Roth (1999) 'The lobby's dying gasps?', *British Journalism Review*, vol. 10, no. 3, pp. 21–4.
4. *Ibid.*
5. Based on Gaber's personal experience in the lobby.
6. *Ibid.*
7. Peter Riddell (1999) 'A shift of power and influence', *British Journalism Review*, vol. 10, no, 33, p. 28.

8. Interview, December 1998.
9. Private conversation.
10. Jackie Ashley (1999) '*New Statesman* profile. The lobby', *New Statesman*, 18 October.
11. Interview, September 1998.
12. This refers to the 'indigenous' press such as the *Scotsman* and the *Herald* in Scotland and the *Western Mail* in Cardiff but not to the Scottish and Welsh editions of the London-based dailies.
13. The select committees monitor the work of government departments and conduct investigations into specific topics; the grand committees are debating chambers for all Scottish and Welsh MPs.
14. Riddell, *op. cit.*, p. 32.
15. Ashley, *op. cit.*
16. Interview, September 1998.
17. Quoted in Nicholas Jones (1999) *Sultans of Spin: The Media and the New Labour Government*, p. 278. London: Gollancz.

CHAPTER TEN

Conclusions: why this crisis is real

The turn of the century is a peculiar time in British politics. A New Labour government with a huge majority, apparently wishing to govern through consensual rather than ideological politics, seems determined to hang on to the centre ground which it captured through a series of policy contortions during the last few years of the twentieth century. Despite the best attempts of party leaders to stoke up the confrontational style that has characterized British politics for generations, it is difficult to identify real ideological differences between the parties. With Europe perhaps the one remaining issue of serious political division, all else is reduced to parties being able to convince the electorate that they will be sufficiently competent and trust-worthy to ensure the continued contentment of the Galbraithian two-thirds while sufficiently compassionate to mitigate any excessive hardship of the remaining third. In the politics of pragmatism and consumerism, presenta-tion assumes a much greater importance than at times of fundamental political division.

For a meaningful analysis of the state of contemporary political journalism, it is therefore important to detach it from the turn-of-the-century political context – or at least to identify which of the current trends and practices are part of a long-term shift rather than a temporary reaction to events. Once the political pendulum begins to swing back towards the Conservative Party – as at some stage is (almost) inevitable – will the forces outlined in this book still be conspiring to degrade the reporting of politics? We believe the answer to be yes, because our arguments transcend fundamental shifts in the political climate. To reinforce the case, however, it is important to answer two converse arguments: first, that changes in party presentational techniques have actually helped to make politics more universally accessible to more people; and second, that technological changes will have an empowering effect which will nullify most of the adverse trends outlined here. In both cases, the argument goes, we are seeing a progressive democratization of political communication.

The first argument has been advanced most recently by Brian McNair.[1] While acknowledging that political journalism has become more entertainment-led, more focused on news management and more spec-ulative than before, he interprets these trends not as evidence of dumbing down, tabloidisation, Americanisation or any of the related terms deployed in the various narratives of decline which characterise cultural pessimism, but as intelligible and in many respects welcome journalistic responses to changes in the technological, economic and political environments which shape political culture.[2]

As examples, McNair interprets a journalistic fixation with the mechanics of news management as a force for transparency and therefore empowerment; a shift towards adversarial coverage as a move away from deference and towards a greater willingness to challenge authority; and the commercial imperative for ratings as a force for creating 'new spaces for the accessing and meaningful representation of non-elite voices'. He is particularly critical of the wholesale condemnation of spin doctoring, on the basis that the practice is centuries old and that at least today's sophisticated techniques are being subjected to equally sophisticated daily scrutiny by the media. While politicians have always manipulated presentation and image, today 'they must do so against the background of a vigilant and often ruthless media, and often in front of a live audience'. On this argument, the subversive power of journalism is the very force for popular (rather than populist) democracy that its critics maintain is rapidly diminishing.

It is incontestable that over the past fifty years journalism has shifted substantially from an unhealthily subservient relationship with politicians to a more equal status. The anecdotes about Churchill refusing to let reporters into Downing Street and prime ministerial briefings under Harold Macmillan and Sir Alec Douglas-Home being run 'in the spirit of the butler at a great country estate addressing the domestic staff' confirm the one-way nature of that relationship until at least the early 1960s.[3] The decline of deference that is manifested in all aspects of modern society, from a genuine constitutional debate about the role and purpose of a monarchy to a healthier scepticism about all areas of 'authority', has certainly infiltrated the realm of political journalism. There is equally no question that the resulting demystification process makes the process of government more transparent and politicians more accountable to a fourth estate which is no longer reluctant to flex its muscles supposedly in the name of the people.

With the eclipse of deference, however, has come a burgeoning power to undermine governments and individual politicians which is perceived – accurately or not – to be more potent and irresponsibly wielded even than in the heyday of Lords Beaverbrook and Northcliffe. The difference today is that reporters do not require the licence of their proprietors to expose or challenge individual politicians (though of course it helps). It is the natural professional order of things. And while that process certainly brings with it greater accountability of politicians to a more sceptical electorate, it also breeds in political parties a sense of foreboding and mistrust that evolves into a siege mentality. Politicians now believe, rightly or wrongly, that the media hold the key to electoral success and that any and every technique is permissible in their determination to convey their message – even if those techniques are inimical to the principles of transparency and proper demo-cratic debate.

In American terms, the media are 'the beast' to be tamed and controlled. Some of the thought processes within the two American parties were revealed in the gripping tale told by two of the main protagonists in the 1992 presidential election, Mary Matalin and James Carville – who were senior members respectively of the Republican and Democratic campaign teams and who subsequently put aside their political differences to get married (to each other). The story each of them told of a political party's relationship with the media was almost identical: consistency and repetition were the watch-words, even if it meant enduring complaints about 'manipulation'. In Matalin's words, 'The absolute rule of message dissemination and message penetration is consistency and repetition. The principle is the same for political campaigns or companies: Everyone says the same thing *over* and *over*.'[4] In her view, this is not just an expedient for dealing with journalists who want to trip up politicians, but an important leadership quality: 'The leadership of this country should be focused, should be able to tell the American people where we're going. A united voice from the administration gives the public a clear view of its direction; clarity gives the public confidence.'

Making the same point, Carville gave a telling example of the importance of consistency in facing persistent questioning from political journalists looking for a story. Having carefully laid out his critique of the economy, Bill Clinton was asked about his draft record by reporters trying to give some new 'legs' to the story that he had avoided being called up for military service in Vietnam. Instead of ignoring them, Clinton urged them to check President Bush's record on the Iran–Contra scandal and drew attention to a conversa-tion between two cabinet members 'which, if true, would call into question not only the President's veracity but his support for illegal conduct'. Carville records his own intense frustration and the reasons why such spontaneity is anathema to the political strategist:

> Now, what do you think is going to get on TV? Do you think in your life it'll be 'Not back to tax and spend but ahead to invest and grow'? Of course not. The Beast don't want to report the stump speech, they hear it all the time; the Beast don't care about the economy, that's boring to them. The Beast likes the draft story, the Beast likes the Democratic nominee saying the incumbent President's 'veracity' is in question. . . . That is why when you watch the news, you will often see a candidate glide right by reporters without stopping. We're happy then. If the candidate doesn't say anything else but what he's supposed to, the media don't have anything to run but what he said.[5]

Both Carville and Matalin were quite clear about their priority during the 1992 campaign, and that this was more than just winning an important election. It was to convey to the electorate via every conceivable communica-tion platform why their candidate was (as each passionately believed) the politician with the character and the programmes which were best for

America; and, conversely, why his opponent was not. All communication with the media was geared to that end and, their argument went, democracy was being served rather than debased by this aggressive and transparent partisanship. In Carville's words,

> One of the things that people should understand is that the whole idea of leaking information and talking to reporters is good. It ain't bad for democracy. It's very much a function of what reporters should do, which is ferret out things people don't know, and what campaigns ought to be doing, which is putting their candidate before the public. We're giving them facts, leads, directions to take, things to go on.[6]

Much the same arguments were propounded in Britain during the 1990s as those who stood accused most often of manipulation and undermining democratic practice answered their critics. In a revealing article at the start of a long run-up to the 1997 British election, Labour's prime strategist, Peter Mandelson, echoed Carville's passionate commitment to the cause and his primary purpose 'to put our principles and values up in lights, fighting a Tory Lie machine'. He pointed to the massive increase in political coverage and the consequent 'search for news' which led to exaggeration or manu-facture of stories about dissent or division which in turn obliged party managers to react with intense caution and rigorously control the outflow of information. And he drew attention to the honourable history of soundbites, going back to Aristotle and even Lenin who had 'distilled the communist manifesto down to the soundbite "Bread, Peace and Land" '.[7] Implicit in the Mandelson message was the view that the onus for preserving good political journalism lay with the practitioners themselves, first to stand up to those whose job was to be passionate about their cause, and second to be more responsible and less sensationalist about the nature of their coverage.

The consequences of this stand-off between a media hungry for political news and a political culture determined to resist 'the Beast' tend not to be the enlightened and empowering public space which McNair promotes. It is worth summarizing the reasons, illustrated throughout this book, why this is so and why our conclusions are so pessimistic.

First, the nature of the power relationship is grossly unequal, making what might otherwise be a productive dialectical approach to political commu-nication increasingly barren. The embattled psychology of modern political parties and their spokespeople means that their techniques in dealing with the media are, in modern parlance, 'robust'. Many of those on the receiving end believe that this robustness is increasingly teetering over the edge into unacceptable intimidation or a non-co-operation which is the antithesis of genuine political debate. We have chronicled some of the examples given by Nicholas Jones, one of the BBC's political reporters, and Peter Oborne talks in his book on Alastair Campbell about the bullying and abuse dealt out on a routine basis by Campbell, Mandelson and their underlings. As Oborne makes clear, this is more than macho posturing. He describes a threat to the editor of one Scottish newspaper whose correspondent had been particularly awkward, which implied that the reporter's lobby status would be removed, 'thus destroying his livelihood'. After a particularly furious row with Sky News political editor Adam Boulton, he ensured that Sky TV 'was frozen out of interviews' when Peter Mandelson resigned the following day.[8]

Some of Britain's most respected political journalists – none of whom can be described as shrinking violets in the face of an overbearing politician - have joined the chorus of concern. James Naughtie of the BBC's *Today* programme has said, 'There is something in the new relationship between ministers and journalists which is irritating. The manipulation can be sinister.'[9] And way back in 1992, the BBC's John Simpson drew an unflattering comparison between American 'spin doctors' and their British counterparts:

> In the United States, the parties try, as they do here, to ensure that the coverage will be as favourable as possible to them; but if it is not they change their own approach. They do not attack the broadcasters nor hint at their possible dissolution.[10]

To some extent this is a problem, as we have seen, which is peculiar to the BBC, and by extension to any country with a substantial publicly funded broadcaster. Given the importance of the BBC as a public space for political debate in the United Kingdom, however, it is becoming a problem for political journalism in general.

Avoidance techniques, as we have seen, are also increasingly common. Almost as soon as it came into office the Blair government engaged in a systematic attempt to minimize public debate on a number of problematic issues by refusing to allow ministers to enter the broadcasting fray. Programmes such as *Newsnight* on BBC2 and ITN's *Channel Four News* found that senior ministers were rarely accepting invitations to be interviewed alongside their critics – they would offer to do a single interview with the presenter or sometimes refuse to appear at all. At the end of 1997 the government faced its first major backbench revolt when 47 Labour MPs voted against cutting benefits to lone-parent families. Throughout the period of that controversy, no Labour minister went into a TV studio with lone parents, representatives of lone-parent organizations, a Liberal Democrat or any Labour backbencher opposed to the measure. Since at the time the Conservatives were supporting the government's position, no effective debate took place on a matter of great public interest. The process was repeated when, following a leaked report suggesting that the government was also about to cut some disability benefits, no minister would agree to appear on television to discuss the issue with representatives of groups campaigning for disabled people.

On any definition of democratic accountability and openness, it is difficult to see positive benefits to such deliberate orchestration. Ironically, the government itself has underlined the need for – and its commitment to – openness in its own White Paper on freedom of information. David Clark, the minister responsible, wrote in the introduction, 'Openness is fundamental to the political health of a modern state'.[11] In one of those further twists that tend to characterize the games theory of today's political communication, the White Paper itself became a victim of the sport of media manipulation. Details were leaked to the BBC two days before its official publication, thus distracting public attention from the government's difficulties over embarrassing revelations about the financial affairs of its Paymaster General. Thus, when David Clark came to launch the White Paper, he was not able to benefit from any positive press coverage, and was even forced to precede his introductory statement to the House of Commons with a grovelling apology for the leak, and a promise of an investigation to root out the culprit!

From the time of its election in 1997, the Labour government was quite brutal in its efforts to control the publicity process. Between its accession to power in May 1997 and December 1999 the government succeeded in removing sixteen of the eighteen most senior press officers in Whitehall. These changes coincided with the creation of a new, centralized information and rebuttal system known as the 'knowledge network', which, according to the *Guardian*, was designed 'to explain the government's core message to the public without going through the distorting prism of media reporting and to ensure that all in Whitehall work off a common script which is instantly capable of being updated'.[12] The project sought to collect, in one database, every news line that ministers and civil servants would need to take on every key government policy, and to provide them with the ammunition to deal with criticism on policy from MPs, the media and the public. Included in the database (a far more powerful tool than Excalibur, which the Labour Party used to drive its 1997 election campaign) were:

- a daily, weekly and medium-term media planning tool (a battle plan);
- comprehensive and concise briefing sheets on departmental activity, top-line themes and messages;
- full texts of key ministerial speeches;
- full texts of departmental press releases;
- a common format for supplying Downing Street with required material for Prime Minister's questions;
- key quotes, key facts and rapid reaction to attacks on departmental policy and practice; and
- instant breakdowns to regional and constituency level of departmental announcements and activity.[13]

The 'knowledge network' was also to be used to build up a database on the government's most persistent critics and sketch out lines to be taken in response. Moreover, for the first time, information was to be routinely broken down by constituencies – an invaluable tool in any subsequent election campaign. The *Guardian* found these proposals worrying. In a leading article, it asked:

And what does the civil service make of it? If it is not alarmed, then it should be, at the implications which pulse through the paper that civil servants – whose right and duty it is not to become mere obedient conduits of government policy – will have that impartiality sapped; will find themselves caught in an exercise appropriate in some respects to a ministry of propaganda. And may not this tastefully named Knowledge Network Project ease gracefully, as the election approaches, into a souped-up version of the Excalibur project which served Labour so well in 1997? Only this time, of course, funded by taxpayers. All governments play these games. But none before in peacetime can have sought to play them so lavishly, making centralisation a religion, trampling on diversity, doing its best to ensure that from Mr Blair down through the government ranks and into the civil service, we are permitted to hear but one voice.[14]

We understand the reasons why a more professionalized and media-literate political party should take every conceivable step to ensure that its policy initiatives and political arguments are conveyed to the electorate in the manner of its choosing, but the scale and all-embracing nature of this operation makes any sensible political communication increasingly difficult. In the words of political commentator Hugo Young,

> As treated by Labour, the press, tabloid and other, is a potent enemy of truth. It has become the reason for silence, rather than the agent of communication. Ask a shadow minister why policy is hedged about with infinite imprecision, and the answer invariably relates to the wicked distortions that would otherwise be applied to it by the liars of Wapping or the Dogs.[15]

This leads directly to the second problem. Any enfranchisement of the electorate through a more vigorous journalistic culture is refracted through media owners who have agendas which will often distort or prevent constructive political discourse. Sometimes, as we have seen, the agenda will be dictated by some kind of legislative or regulatory favour being sought by owners, at other times by a political or ideological framework, at still others by straightforward commercial imperatives. When the *Sun* famously stuck a picture of Prime Minister Tony Blair – whom it vigorously supported in the election a year earlier – on the front page with the headline 'Is THIS the most dangerous man in Britain?', it was following Rupert Murdoch's committed anti-single currency line, which makes any informed journalism about Europe a virtual impossibility in that newspaper.[16] Similar criticisms have been made about the *Daily Telegraph*, whose reputation for impartial news coverage has rapidly diminished in the face of committed editorial lines on rejecting peace proposals for Ulster, opposing the European single currency and opposing constitutional reform of the House of Lords. According to one experienced commentator, 'Even its severest critics have always conceded that the "Torygraph's" news columns were straight. Now, particularly on such defining issues as Europe, Ulster and the House of Lords, *Telegraph* reports have been slanted to suit the Editor's political line.'[17] In the *Telegraph*'s case it was the editor rather than the owner who took the initiative, but the consequences for news reporting remain the same.

Commercial advantage, as we have seen, can also play a crucial role in determining the nature and content of political journalism. The ability of an owner to be brutal in protecting his commercial interests was graphically illustrated by Rupert Murdoch in February 1998 when he ordered his publishing division, HarperCollins, to stop publication of a book by the former governor of Hong Kong, Chris Patten, for which the company had signed a £125,000 contract. Patten, a respected cabinet minister in the Conservative government before 1992, was strongly critical of China. Unfortunately, Murdoch had extensive television interests in South-East Asia and was determined to make inroads into the highly lucrative Chinese market. The book's sentiments conflicted with his corporate priorities, and was sacrificed to commercial expedience. In a daily newspaper such decisions are rarely so blatant or premeditated: rather, they are incremental, often involving attempts by reporters to second-guess their news editors and editors. Occasionally, commercial self-interest dictates a news and editorial line which is breathtakingly contemptuous of government and politicians. When, in February 1999, a Conservative member of the European Parliament was revealed by the press to have brought in some cannabis and gay pornography from the Continent, Tony Blair could not conceal his frustration with the scandal-mongering tabloids and threatened to 'take on the press'. The clear implication was a much-touted privacy act which many observers believe to be long overdue in the UK. The *Sun* reacted with the kind of vitriol at which it excels:

> Too many politicians are sad, sordid, pathetic, inadequate wimps with private lives that make ordinary people's stomachs churn. They are not fit to hold office. So, Mr Blair, get your tank off our lawn. Remember that we speak for millions of Brits who live cleaner lives than half of Westminster. We speak for the people who put you and your fornicating friends into power.[18]

Apart from an overt reminder of the bloody battle that would inevitably follow any attempt to pursue privacy legislation and thus curtail a journalistic licence which is the bread and butter of a tabloid newspaper like the *Sun*, such language does little to enhance the reputation of politicians or interest in political reporting. When the marketplace is as crowded and ferocious as that in which the British tabloid press operates, there is little room for the niceties of protecting private lives.

This, in turn, leads to the third problem, which embraces not just the tabloid press but every aspect of the media world: proliferation and competition. We have detailed the massive increase in news outlets, whether through newsprint, more opportunities on existing radio or television channels, new cable and satellite channels or online services. If each incremental addition to the media mix were to produce a concomitant increase in the number of working journalists and the amount of resources being invested in reporting politics, no one could complain. If anything, the opposite appears to be happening. In almost every area of news production, the number of journalists is being reduced, opportunities for permanent employment are diminishing and being replaced by an uncommitted freelance culture, training is being cut, and existing journalists are being asked to service an increasing number of outlets. The growth of electronic forms of communication, while offering plenty of new opportunities to complement and compete with traditional media, has also stretched the resources of traditional media companies, which have all started their own electronic enterprises to preempt the competition. Thus, an already severely curtailed investment in journalism has been squeezed still further by the very technological developments which were supposed to be liberating.

The problem is compounded, even more ironically, by the proliferation of information being made available. The sheer quantity of information flowing out of Whitehall departments has been growing rapidly. In 1999 government departments issued around 13,500 press releases, more than 3,000 up on the previous year (the first full one for the Labour government) figure of 10,300. This compared with just under 8,000 in 1997, 7,400 in 1996 and 5,700 in 1995.[19] And the size of the Downing Street press and media machine has increased from an average personnel of around six under previous governments to around 25 in 2000, operating on a virtual 24-hour basis.[20] Here, it could be argued, is proof of a government truly committed to placing ever greater quantities of information into the public domain and thus fulfilling its commitment towards more open government.

There are two problems with this process. First, too much information can stifle the news production process almost as effectively as too little. The more information there is, the harder it becomes – particularly in the context of 24-hour news operations – for journalists to distinguish the valuable from the mundane, and the more tempting it becomes to look for the 'guidance' which press officers are all too willing to supply. Second, it becomes far more difficult for journalists to identify the information which, while not being factually incorrect, is certainly presented in a deliberately misleading fashion. A good example was presented in a BBC *Panorama* programme in March 2000 which detailed how a single £20 million injection of funds into the National Health Service had been announced by the government on four separate occasions: in September 1998, November 1998, April 1999 and September 1999. None of the press notices which accompanied these announcements revealed that this was the same money which had been previously publicized. According to the programme's editor, Peter Horrocks, 'Whitehall civil servants have told *Panorama* that such statements are always cleared directly by ministers, who are keen that the words "modernised", "beacon", "extra" and "boost" are frequently used.'[21]

Increasingly it is being left to the BBC to pursue the kind of investigative journalism required to sift through the barrage of information to find a story. The problem, inevitably, is money. Journalism which is deprived of investment inevitably becomes journalism which is more reliant on the never-ending stream of press releases from PR departments. And just as investment in corporate PR has burgeoned in almost inverse proportion to the resources devoted to independent journalism, so – as we have seen – the effort invested by political parties in their own public relations has expanded while financial commitment to political journalism has at best remained static. To put it more bluntly, there are the same number of journalists working longer hours to feed more outlets and with proportionately less time for finding things out and challenging the wisdoms or 'facts' handed down by governments, oppositions or well-funded pressure groups. Writing recently in the *Guardian*, one of the BBC's most fiercely independent journalists, Jeremy Paxman, put it succinctly with a simple rule that 'good journalism is bad business and too often bad journalism is good business'. Bad journalism is a question not just of getting facts wrong, but of having neither the time nor the inclination to follow a different agenda or create rather than follow stories. Paxman continued:

> Finding things out, as anyone who has done any investigative journalism knows, takes time, and time is money. Resources are now so stretched on some newsdesks that no one can spare the time to research a story properly. The consequence is that they are increasingly dependent on what they are told. . . . It is our job to find out things that people do not want to have found out. But for journalists to function properly, they have to be given freedom and resources. And those will come only from organisations which believe that their first duty is disclosure, not entertainment.[22]

This is why, in the end, we are pessimistic about the future of political journalism and cannot share McNair's positive interpetation that we are in fact seeing 'the emergence of a demystificatory, potentially empowering commentary on the nature of the political process . . . which adds to rather than detracts from the stock of useful information available to the average citizen'.[23] It is worth referring back to the coverage of the sacking of Charlie Whelan, then Press Secretary to the Chancellor of the Exchequer, in January 1999. This story was widely covered throughout the media on the day of the sacking and its ramifications further examined in the broadsheet press and by broadcasters over the next few days. What did the 'average' reader of the tabloid press make of this voluminous coverage about the resignation of what to many must have appeared a minor government functionary? For while those with an obsessive interest in politics were fascinated by the machinations that preceded Whelan's resignation (see Chapters 7 and 8) and what it told us about the tension between a Prime Minister and his Chancellor, did it really empower the average citizen? The same goes for all the revelations about Tony Blair's obsession with image outlined in our Introduction and the burgeoning number of unflattering profiles of his Press Secretary, Alastair Campbell. All these might reveal the machinery of modern publicity to the public gaze, but what information was displaced which might have told the average citizen more about government initiatives being planned for, say, more formal testing of school pupils, for stricter rules on asylum seekers, for a reorganization of hospitals or for a wholesale restructuring of the benefits system?

Our complaint in the end is not that politicians have a surfeit of power which is incapable of challenge by good journalists operating on an equal footing, or that there is too much emphasis on presentation or process by governments. Our complaint is that, for all the reasons detailed in this book and summarized eloquently by Jeremy Paxman, the kind of interrogative, painstaking and oppositional journalism which is required to invigorate the public sphere and assist citizens in a democracy in understanding the nature of the problems their elected representatives are tackling – and their success or otherwise in dealing with them – is being progressively undermined. Journalists as a professional class are probably better qualified and better equipped for their task than ever before; the presentational strategies of governments and parties are probably better understood and deconstructed than ever before. But these undoubted advances over the political journalism of fifty years ago do little to overcome the combined impediments of competition, proliferation of news sources, business priorities of media owners, and political PR. Even more depressing is the undoubted fact that each of these impediments will, over the years to come, become even more severe and make the task of even the most determinedly independent political journalist that much more difficult.

Notes

1. Brian McNair (2000) *Journalism and Democracy: An Evaluation of the Political Public Sphere.* London: Routledge.
2. McNair, *op. cit.*, p. 171.
3. Peter Oborne (1999) *Alastair Campbell: New Labour and the Rise of the Media Class.* London: Aurum Press.
4. Mary Matalin and James Carville (1994) *All's Fair: Love, War and Running for President,* p. 80. New York: Random House.
5. *Op. cit.*, p. 328.
6. *Op. cit.*, p. 431.
7. 'Out of the darkness', *Guardian, The Week,* 28 September 1996, p. 1.
8. Oborne, *op. cit.*, p. 182.
9. Petronella Wyatt, 'Don't you dare call me dour', *Daily Telegraph,* 28 May 1998, p. 25.
10. John Simpson, 'A nasty and menacing election', *The Spectator,* 28 March 1992, pp. 9–10.
11. The Stationery Office, 1997, *Your Right to Know: The Government's Proposals for a Freedom of Information Act,* Cmd 3818, p. 4.
12. *Guardian,* 7 January 2000.
13. *Ibid.*
14. *Ibid.*
15. Hugo Young, 'Running scared of the tabloids', *Guardian,* 25 June 1996, p. 17.
16. *Sun,* 24 June 1998, p. 1. Blair denied that he subsequently adopted a softer line on the single currency, but some commentators detected a more ambivalent approach in the weeks that followed.
17. Brian Macarthur, 'Is the Telegraph losing its touch?', *The Times 3,* 3 December 1999, p. 47. Given that *The Times* is owned by Murdoch and sees the *Telegraph* as its closest rival, this would not normally be regarded as a strictly impartial judgement. However, similar observations were made by Hugo Young in the *Guardian* and Professor Ian Hargreaves of Cardiff University, formerly editor of the *Independent*.
18. *Sun,* 1 February 1999, p. 8.

Index